Understanding
HORSE
BEHAVIOUR

Understanding
HORSE
BEHAVIOUR

Lesley Skipper

NEW
HOLLAND

First published in 2007 by
New Holland Publishers (UK) Ltd
London • Cape Town • Sydney • Auckland

Garfield House, 86–88 Edgware Road, London
W2 2EA, United Kingdom
www.newhollandpublishers.com

80 McKenzie Street, Cape Town 8001, South Africa

Level 1, Unit 4, 14 Aquatic Drive, Frenchs Forest,
NSW 2086, Australia

218 Lake Road, Northcote, Auckland, New Zealand

ISBN: 978 1 84537 603 1

Senior Editor: Sarah Goulding
Design: Stonecastle Graphics Ltd
Illustrations: Maggie Raynor
Production: Marion Storz
Publishing Director: Rosemary Wilkinson

10 9 8 7 6 5 4 3 2 1

Reproduction by Modern Age Repro House Ltd
Printed and bound by Craft Print International
Ltd, Singapore

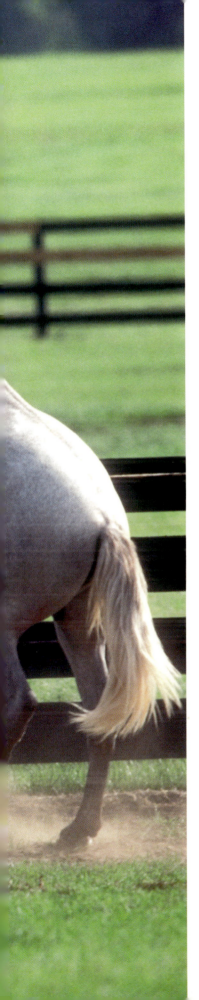

Contents

Introduction

T HE LAST few decades have seen enormous progress in our understanding of equine behaviour. As well as various scientific studies designed to improve our knowledge of how horses behave in domestic settings, a number of long-term studies have been carried out on horses living in wild or semi-wild conditions.

In spite of this, it is all too easy for us to forget that the behaviour of horses is adapted to a free-ranging lifestyle in very different environments from those in which domestic horses are usually kept. Not so very long ago they were seen as having been set upon earth purely to serve us, and even now there are still some trainers who believe they have (in the words of one such trainer) a 'God-given right to dominate the horse'. This has led to many people behaving as though horses exist purely for our convenience and simply ignoring or overriding the animal's psychological and emotional needs.

However, increasing numbers of horse-owners and horse-lovers are accepting that in return for what the horse gives us, we must ensure we satisfy its psychological and behavioural needs as far as we can. This is not a question of sentimentality but of ethical responsibility. More and more people – including many scientists who previously rejected such ideas – are starting to accept that horses, like other animals, are sentient beings with thoughts, needs and feelings. The acknowledgement that animals are sentient beings is enshrined in the 1997 European Treaty, and it is only a matter of time before non-European countries follow suit.

This new perception of horses as thinking, feeling creatures has been strengthened by the work of a number of open-minded scientists such as Dr Marthe Kiley-Worthington, now based in France, and Dr Evelyn Hanggi, in the USA. In independent studies and experiments they have

Above: At one time horses suffered and died in the service of armies; their place in the military is now purely ceremonial.

Opposite: Horses are no longer simply the servants of humans but heavy horse turnouts such as these are popular at agricultural shows, recalling the days when horse transport was an essential part of everyday life.

Above: Horses continue to serve humans in a variety of ways. All over the world police forces make extensive use of horses; those shown here are on duty at a large agricultural show.

confirmed that horses are capable of learning and understanding far more than we have usually given them credit for, and that if given the chance they lead rich emotional and social lives that reflect the fact that as mammals, they have brains and nervous systems very similar to ours.

Yet all too often this is not recognised because of the lingering perception, common in many quarters and perhaps born of the prejudices outlined above, that horses are creatures of limited brain-power and emotional capacity, with only a few very basic needs. Due to this ignorance, too many horses are subjected to conditions and training regimes that create excessive amounts of stress. Many horse-owners and trainers fail to take the horse's psychological needs into account, and even in those cases where these needs *are* considered, all too often that consideration is based on inaccurate perceptions and information. The result is that far too many horses develop behavioural problems that could have been avoided had the animal's basic physical and psychological needs been taken into account.

If we want to keep horses happy and healthy in a domestic situation and help them cope with all the demands we make on them, we must understand how different situations affect them and how this is expressed in their behaviour. Instead of thinking in terms of horses having 'behaviour problems', we should realize that these problems are usually the result of how we keep our horses and the kind of things we ask of them. Once we understand this we can anticipate problems and in all likelihood prevent them arising in the first place.

The aim of this book is to help horse-owners and horse-lovers understand how domestic life – and the many demands we make of our horses, especially in training and competition – affect their behaviour and their psychological wellbeing. Understanding our horses' behavioural and psychological needs will help us fulfil our ethical responsibilities and in doing so, enable us to enjoy happier, healthier relationships with our horses.

Below: Nowadays horses are ridden mainly for pleasure.

Chapter 1

How stress affects horses

T HE ABILITY of horses to adapt to the demands made upon them by humans – and to widely differing conditions – is an aspect of their nature that has made their use possible in a multitude of ways. In fact, it is difficult to imagine how we could have reached our current levels of technological progress without the horse. Agriculture, transport, communications, land exploration, wars of conquest... all of these would scarcely have been possible without the horse. Yet although this physical and behavioural flexibility has been of immense value to humans, it has been considerably less advantageous to horses. They have been compelled to adapt to a wide variety of management systems, which have usually been designed with the convenience of humans in mind rather than that of the horses themselves. In some cases their adaptability has been stretched to the limit, as many management regimes deprive them of the ability to perform many of their natural behaviours. We will look at these behaviours in the next chapter, but for now let us consider what happens when everyday life produces stresses that individual horses are unable to handle.

What is stress?

In itself, stress is neither good nor bad. Hans Selye, pioneer in stress research, defined it as 'the non-specific response of the body to any demand'. Hormones released into the bloodstream by the endocrine glands or specialized nerve cells regulate this response and tell the body what to do in specific circumstances. For example, if danger threatens, the adrenal glands secrete adrenaline, which increases breathing rate and heart activity and intensifies muscle power. This prepares the body either to stand and fight or to flee – the famous 'fight or flight' syndrome. Stress can therefore be a catalyst in raising the body's energy levels, reducing its reaction time and enhancing the senses' sensitivity. In the short term this can be beneficial as it enhances the body's ability to deal with demanding situations. However, when the long-term demands on an individual exceed that individual's ability to cope with them, stress ceases to be beneficial and becomes *distress*.

The impact of long-term stress on physical health

Long-term stress can affect physical health in many ways. For example, the stress response can increase acid secretions in the stomach, which may in turn increase the risk of gastric and duodenal ulcers. Some of the hormones and neurotransmitters (chemicals enabling the transmission of nerve impulses) produced during those stress responses have been proved to affect the immune system. The temporary suppression of the immune system, which results from the release of these hormones, may act, in the short term, to conserve the energy required for action appropriate to the crisis. But if the stress is constant, the effects on the immune system may be long lasting, leaving the body vulnerable to all manner of viral and bacterial infections.

Below: Colic, especially if it keeps recurring, is a common symptom of chronic stress.

Behavioural problems

Behavioural problems may also arise where stress levels exceed the ability to cope. An increase in aggression, general irritability, and the development of stereotypical behaviour (see Chapter 2, pages 36–38) are common responses, and we can see any or all of these signs in horses that are under stress.

So, how do we know that these are responses to stress, and not caused by something else? Well, we can observe the animals in question in a variety of environments and note how their behaviour differs in each case. If, for example, a high proportion of horses in a specific environment develop similar behavioural problems, we may suspect they are linked to that environment. If the behavioural problems are alleviated or cured completely by a change of environment and/or management regime,

Below: This little foal, temporarily separated from her dam, is showing signs of stress, visible in the tautness of her upper lip.

then that suggests very strongly that our suspicions were correct. Hence, behavioural scientists will try to gather as much information as they can before concluding that 'X' (where 'X' might be a specific situation or environment) is a significant cause of stress in horses.

Studying stress

Another way that scientists can study stress in horses is by taking blood samples at various times and analysing them for the chemicals and hormones which play a key role in the body's response to stress. So although we cannot ask horses directly whether they are suffering from stress, we can observe their behaviour. Then, using the knowledge gained from the various scientific studies carried out on stress in horses and other animals, we can judge whether specific behaviours are the result of stress or whether they stem from some other cause.

Below: The big bay gelding, taken by surprise, is showing alarm at the yearling colt's boisterous approach, even though the colt is not being aggressive.

The stresses of living in the wild

Horses living in the wild have to cope with different kinds of stresses from those experienced by horses living in a domestic setting. Although much has been written about the horse as a prey animal, there are actually very few places in the world where feral (domestic horses living in a wild state) or free-ranging horses face a significant amount of danger from predators. In some parts of the northwest USA the mountain lion (*Felis concolor*), also known as the puma, panther or cougar, may sometimes prey on foals and/or sick and weakened horses. Bears may also sometimes attack horses, although they are not generally a significant risk to feral horses in the USA. Africa's zebras, which are equids and belong to the horse family, may be attacked by large predators such as lions, leopards or hyenas and, when crossing rivers or drinking, by crocodiles. In general, though, large predators capable of bringing down a horse are not common in the lands inhabited by feral horses.

Stallions must surely find the effort of protecting their family against intruders very stressful at times.

Shortage of food and water may produce what is called nutritional stress. Nevertheless, except in times of extreme drought even the horses inhabiting areas such as the Namib Desert manage to stay comparatively healthy in spite of the harshness of their environment.

Feral horses do not defend fixed territories, but the family groups (or 'bands', as such groups are generally called) that constitute feral populations do have home ranges consisting of loosely defined areas within which all their daily activities take place. It is not uncommon for these home ranges to overlap with those of other bands, and the presence of another band inside the home range is generally tolerated. However, in some situations feral horses may be stressed by the incursion of strange horses into their home range, especially if the 'invader' is a stallion attempting to take over a family group. If the newcomer deposes the band's stallion, the new stallion may harass the band mares until they all get to know each other. This process, together with the loss of their own stallion, might conceivably produce high levels of stress in the band mares and their offspring. Stallions, too, must surely find the effort of protecting their family against intruders very stressful at times. However, these are likely to be short-term situations that do not arise every day. In general, feral horses left to their own devices appear to live relatively stress-free lives. Certainly, the kind of stereotyped behaviours usually referred to as 'stable vices', such as weaving, crib-biting, wind-sucking and so on, and which result from long-term stress (which we shall discuss in the next chapter), have not to date been observed in the wild.

Chronic ill health

Among horses in a domestic setting, chronic ill health such as frequent viral infections, loss of appetite with no apparent cause, repeated bouts of colic and gastric ulcers, may be a result of long-term stress. In fact, research carried out in Hong Kong, the USA, Australia and the UK suggests that a startlingly high number of horses used for racing and competition may be affected by gastric ulcers; the figures may be as high as 90 per cent of racehorses and up to 60 per cent of show and competition horses. Ulcers are caused by an excess of acid in the upper part of the horse's stomach, which – unlike the lower portion of the equine stomach – is not well protected against the acids and enzymes that help to break down food. The main reason why racehorses, show and competition horses suffer such a high incidence of ulcers is that so many of them spend a high proportion of their time stabled up with limited amounts of forage to eat. A regular intake of feed such as grass, hay or alfalfa (lucerne) helps to neutralize stomach acids. However, horses engaged in hard work are usually fed a diet high in grain, which actually stimulates the gastric secretions that cause ulcers.

Although diet and prolonged periods without food are common causes of gastric ulcers in horses, stressful environments and the stresses associated with intensive training can also be factors. High levels of exercise decrease blood flow to the stomach, which lowers its protection against acid secretions. Travelling, changes of environment, lack of companionship, being turned out with incompatible companions and so on can all create sufficient stress to cause an increase in stomach acids, leading to the formation of ulcers. Weanlings are especially susceptible to ulcers because even when they are allowed to graze almost continually, the stress of separation from their mothers can create an acid build-up in the stomach. In some cases this build-up may even lead to perforating ulcers and death.

Racehorses, show and competition horses suffer a high incidence of ulcers because so many of them spend a high proportion of their time stabled up with limited amounts of forage to eat.

Behavioural symptoms of stress

Where stress affects mental health, both physical symptoms and behavioural problems commonly arise, but the form these take varies from species to species. So what kind of behavioural problems might we expect to see arising from stress in horses? Many of the problems listed are routinely attributed to a faulty temperament or inadequate training, yet they may all be symptoms of stress created by an inappropriate environment, and training and/or management practices.

These problems include:

An increase in aggression towards other horses: This may include chasing, biting, kicking or frequent threats of such actions and this is atypical behaviour as horses are generally peaceable creatures. In the wild, aggression is generally limited to specific situations – for example between rival stallions, or mares with new foals reacting to the close presence of other mares. Unprovoked aggression in a domestic setting may, however, be evidence of a potentially serious management problem.

Aggression towards humans: This is often attributed to a faulty temperament, yet in a very high proportion of cases it is actually the result of bad experiences with humans, whether in the present or in the past, or to an inadequate or inappropriate environment.

Below: Aggression to other horses can be a sign of environmental stress.

Irritability and general bad temper: This may include grumpiness in the stable; reluctance to co-operate when being groomed, tacked up, ridden and so on, but may also be caused by acute or chronic pain.

Tension evident in body language: Look for muscles that are hard and taut (the muscles on a fit horse should be firm without being hard and unyielding), tension in the muscles around the eyes and mouth, laid-back ears, rolling eyes and the tail being swished about violently (this can be distinguished by its intensity from the more leisurely kind of tail swish that drives away flies). In this situation, the horse will lash its tail up and down, from side to side or in a circular motion with considerable violence, an action that is repeated for as long as the horse feels tense and upset.

So-called stable 'vices': These are not vices at all; they are simply the horse's attempt to alleviate frustration at being unable to perform certain behaviours. They include crib-biting, wind-sucking, weaving, head-nodding and box-walking. These stereotypies, as they are known, are discussed in Chapter 2, pages 36–38.

Above: Aggression to humans may be a response to previous bad experiences with humans, or it may be a response to an inadequate environment. This mare is protecting her personal space.

Pacing about in the field: Some horses may show no stereotyped behaviour in the stable, yet spend a great deal of time pacing about or walking in circles when out in the field. This is a sign that the horse is uncomfortable with something in its field environment, and being turned out with incompatible companions is a common cause of this kind of stress. Alternatively, the horse may also be bothered by something in the turnout environment. For instance, the close proximity of something the horse finds worrying, such as non-equine animals like dogs, insect pests or noisy machinery nearby could upset it – the possibilities are many and only close and frequent observation will shed light on what actually is bothering the horse.

Reluctance to move: When the horse is reluctant to leave the stable, move around in the field, or under saddle, pain could be the reason so it is important that this is always investigated as a possible cause.

'Switching off': The horse may be obedient, but performs what is asked of it in a mechanical, zombie-like manner.

Opposite: Tail swishing can be an indication that the horse is tense and upset. This Arabian stallion is annoyed by the close presence of other stallions in the showring.

Below: This circle was worn by horses pacing. Although several horses were involved, the circle was mainly trodden by one mare who was stressed by the presence of uncongenial companions.

Situations that can create stress

So, what kinds of situations create stress in horses to the extent that individuals react in some or all of the ways described above? Some of the primary causes of stress in horses are given below and these are all discussed more fully in later chapters:

Early and/or abrupt weaning: Foals need the comfort and security of their mother's presence for much longer than conventional weaning practices allow.

Confinement to a stable for long periods: The horse is unable to fulfil its need to move around and to perform its normal eating behaviour.

Isolation from companions for prolonged periods: As a social species horses need companionship.

Insufficient forage: Horses have digestive systems geared to long spells of eating so lack of forage for any length of time may cause digestive upsets, ulcers and stereotyped behaviour.

Below: Suckling does not just satisfy nutritional needs, it can also be comfort-seeking behaviour, as in the case of this nine-month-old foal.

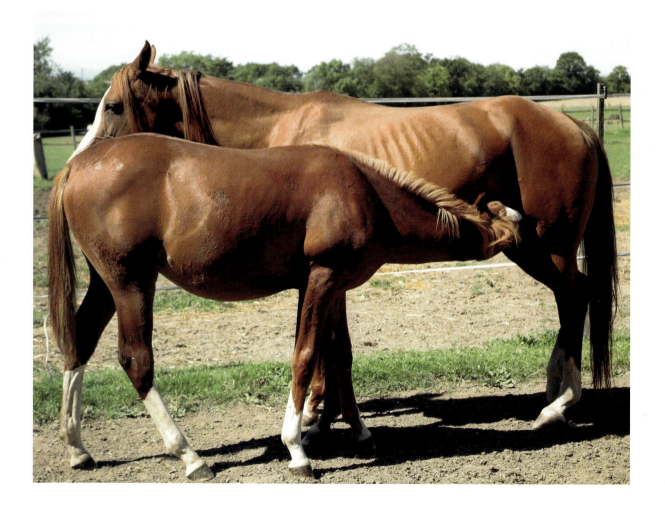

Over-feeding cereals: High-energy feed coupled with insufficient exercise may create behavioural problems such as excitability, general restlessness, explosiveness under saddle (such as bucking, shying or bolting) or cause gastric ulcers.

Over- or under-stimulation: If the horse is stabled, the environment may be too 'busy' for it (too many things going on – loud noises, people shouting or talking loudly, dogs barking, for example) and it may be unable to get sufficient rest. Or, the environment may be barren, with insufficient activity to keep it interested.

Being turned out with hostile or aggressive companions: Although horses need companionship, in many domestic situations they are confined to comparatively small areas and may be unable to escape if harassed.

Coercive training: This, or methods that rely too heavily on 'negative reinforcement' (see Chapter 4, pages 64–65) or on inappropriate concepts of what is important to horses, can cause problems. Even among experienced trainers there is a great deal of confusion regarding what constitutes 'natural' behaviour for horses.

Over-training: The horse is regularly pushed to or beyond the limits of its physical and mental abilities.

Use of punishment in training: Many people are confused about learning processes and may be using punishment without being aware that this is *actually* what they are doing.

Inconsistency in training and handling: Trainers and handlers may punish or reward the horse for a specific action one day but not the next.

Confusing signals from handler/rider: This is especially common in ridden work as riders may be giving the horse conflicting instructions (for example, by kicking the horse to make it move while pulling back on the reins).

Over-training prior to competition: For many people success in competition is so important that they forget that the horse is not a machine but has its physical and mental limits, just as we do.

Too high a frequency of competition: Some horses adapt to the demands of competition better than others.

Failure in competition: A rider or trainer should **never** take their frustration and disappointment out on the horse. Although horses are far more intelligent than they are usually thought to be, they cannot be expected to share human ambitions or to understand why competition is so important to their trainers/riders.

Bad experiences while travelling: Poor driving habits, insufficient room in the horsebox/trailer, loss of balance and claustrophobia all contribute to a fear of travelling because it makes the horse feel insecure.

Even among experienced trainers there is a great deal of confusion regarding what constitutes 'natural' behaviour for horses.

Above: This horse's fear of the fence is evident in his taut muzzle and slightly rolled back eye.

Frequent long journeys: Some horses, especially seasoned competition horses, may grow accustomed to travelling long distances and take it in their stride, but some never do and the process may increase stress levels beyond the individual's ability to cope.

Unrealistic demands: These may be made as a result of a handler/trainer/rider's preconceived ideas about specific breeds/types of horse. Breed stereotypes abound, leading many people to assume that **all** members of a breed will behave/react to training in the same way.

The fact that a situation causes stress is not in itself cause for alarm. Like humans, most horses that are otherwise in good health appear to be quite capable of dealing with moderate amounts of short-term stress. It is when stress becomes severe and/or prolonged that both physical and mental health become compromised. One major factor that has emerged from studies of stress in humans is that the ability to cope with stress is linked to the degree of control the individual has over the situations that create the stress. This is one reason why high-flying executives are often able to cope with higher levels of stress than those in lowlier positions. The executives are likely to have much more say in how their work is structured and to be able to control how they carry it out. They may also have greater job security. Workers at the lower end of the scale may have very little control over what happens to them at work. In addition they may be paid low wages and have little job security – both potential causes of stress.

Horses have little if any control over how their lives are managed, which means that their ability to deal with stress is greatly reduced; after all, they don't have the option of resigning to go to a better owner, for instance. As with humans, however, how a particular horse responds to stress depends very much on that individual and some have (or can develop) better resources for coping than others. As we have seen, there is any number of ways in which we can unwittingly create stress in our horses. Some of these are the result of unquestioned management practices devised for our convenience rather than with the welfare of the horse in mind. Others are caused by insufficient understanding on the part of handlers, trainers and riders, of some of the most fundamental aspects of equine behaviour.

Most horse-owners want to do the best they can for their charges but in many cases cannot due to a lack of knowledge and/or lack of flexibility in training and management regimes. Some practices have come to be taken for granted to the extent that attempts to question or change them may be met with a great deal of resistance from many of the very people who have the power to change them. Yet if those resisting change would only stop to consider the cost – both in terms of equine suffering and of the financial consequences of stress-related illnesses and behavioural problems – they would surely become convinced of the need to make those changes.

Horses, like humans, refuse to conform to rigid ideas on how they should behave and how they should react to specific situations. It is almost 6000 years since horses were first domesticated but we are still very far from knowing everything about what is important to them and essential to their wellbeing. Ideas about equine behaviour have changed as scientific studies have taught us more about how horses and their close relatives live in a wild state, yet the more we learn, the more we realize how much there is still to learn. However, if we use the knowledge we do have, judiciously and with the welfare of the horse in mind, we can hopefully avoid or minimize some of the behavioural problems that arise as a result of our enduring relationship with the horse.

Horses, like humans, refuse to conform to rigid ideas on how they should behave and how they should react to specific situations.

Chapter 2

The importance of natural behaviours to horses

I N CHAPTER 1 we saw how stress can affect horses and that stressful situations arise from the manner in which horses are kept in a domestic setting. They are most likely to suffer from chronic stress when they are deprived of the ability to perform their natural behaviours. But what are these, and how do horses attempt to alleviate stress caused by their suppression?

Before we examine this aspect, however, first let us take a brief look at the origins of the horse of today...

Ancestors of the domestic horse

The remote ancestors (*Hyracotherium*) of the horse were small mammals little bigger than a medium-sized dog, living in the forests of North America and Europe during the Eocene Epoch, between 57 and 52 million years ago. They browsed on low-growing branches of trees, shrubs and shrubby forest plants, but although they were forest-dwellers they were already well adapted for running, with hind legs that were longer than their forelegs.

Opposite: Equid family tree.

Over the next 26 million years or so various ancestral forms of horse flourished; one of them, *Parahippus*, which appeared around 26 million years ago, was the first to resemble modern horses by having teeth adapted to eating grass rather than leaves. Grass is much coarser than the leaves of trees and shrubs and its silica content wears teeth down. Equine teeth have extremely long crowns, which in young horses lie mostly below the gum line. The crown continues to grow out as the grinding surface is worn down; without this continual growth, the teeth would wear down too quickly and before long the horse would be unable to eat. In fact this is precisely what happens to very old horses; their teeth

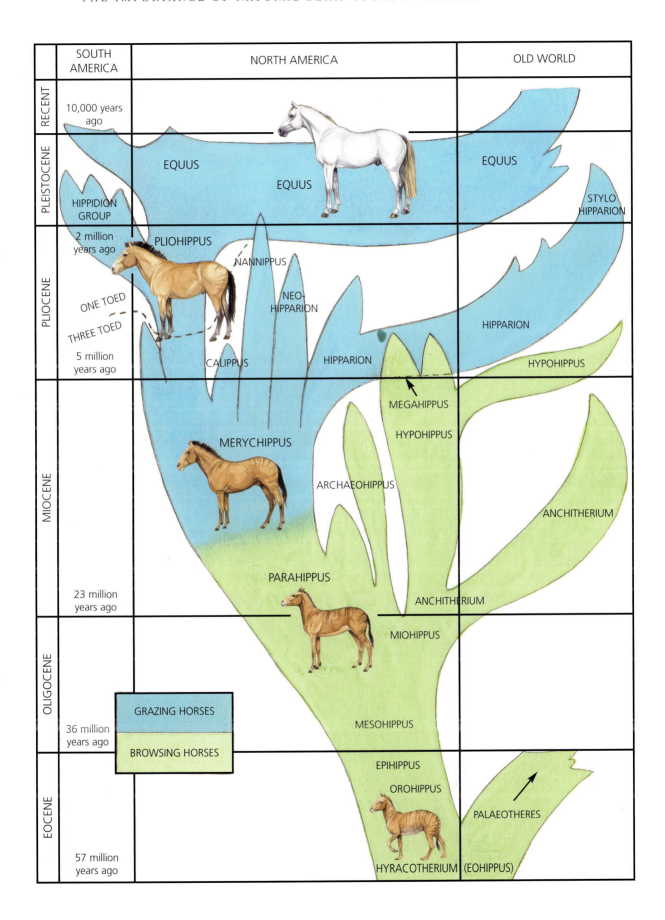

continue to wear down but eventually there is no more crown to grow out. The development of these specialized grinding teeth marked the change from browsing to grazing, and as horses increasingly inhabited grasslands rather than forests, other aspects of their anatomy changed too.

Later ancestors of the modern horse were even better adapted for running than their predecessors. Between around 16 and 5 million years ago another ancestral form of the horse evolved, and this was much more like a modern horse. Standing about 10 hands high, *Merychippus* had some of the limb features of the modern horse. Although this species had three toes, the central toe was enlarged and attached by strong ligaments, which enabled the hoof to spring up and forward powerfully after hitting the ground.

From *Merychippus* descended *Pliohippus*, which lived from about 7 to 2.5 million years ago. *Pliohippus* was the direct ancestor of all modern horses, including asses and zebras as well as the domestic horse, *Equus caballus*, which first appeared around 2.5 million years ago. So we can see that horses have been adapted to grazing and running for many millions of years and their deeply ingrained natural behaviours reflect this.

Social animals

Horses are social animals that in a wild state live in small, relatively stable family groups or 'bands'. A considerable amount of their lives is spent in social interaction, so this too is an important aspect of their natural behaviour.

But how do we know what the natural behaviours of horses may be, when there are no truly wild horses left? The only wild species of *Equus* are the wild asses and zebras and the closest relative of the domestic horse, Przewalski's horse (*Equus przewalskii*), was last recorded in the wild in 1947. However, it is not, as was once thought, a direct ancestor of *E. caballus* but instead has been shown to be a very close cousin. So, although all these species are closely related, how do we know whether their behaviour resembles that of the wild ancestors of our modern horses?

The answer is that we don't. All we can do is look at the behaviour of wild asses, zebras and those herds of Przewalski's horse that have been released back into the wild, and compare their behaviour to see what

Horses are social animals that in a wild state live in small, relatively stable family groups or 'bands'.

aspects are common to all species. We can also – and this is the most valuable source of all – study the behaviour of the various populations of feral horses that live in various parts of the world. These are domestic horses living in a wild state. There are many such populations, and while they all have much in common, we tend to find that various aspects of their behaviour vary according to the local environment and climate. So the best populations to study are those that have had least interference from humans, and have essentially been left to 'do their own thing'.

By combining information from all these sources we can learn a great deal about what matters to horses and what behaviours are essential to their wellbeing. Let us now have a look at these behaviours and see what happens when horses are deprived of the ability to perform them.

Feeding behaviour

As we have seen, horses were originally browsing animals that evolved into grazers, an adaptation that served them well when climate changes resulted in the development of vast grassy plains around 20 million years ago. Studies of bands of feral horses have shown that in the wild horses

Below: The remote ancestors of horses browsed on forest trees and shrubs. Although modern horses are principally grazing animals, they do still like to browse on trees and hedges.

may travel a considerable distance in a day doing nothing more than grazing. They effectively eat on the move and if you watch a group of horses grazing in a field they will seldom stay in one spot for more than a few seconds.

Horses are often referred to as 'trickle-feeders' because although they have very long intestines, their stomachs are comparatively small and are structured so as to cope better with a more or less continual intake of small amounts of food. Feral and free-ranging horses, and those kept out at grass, spend 60 per cent or more of their time eating when the grazing is good. In winter, or on poor pasture, this period may increase by as much as 70 to 80 per cent. On the other hand stabled horses fed a diet rich in cereals but low in forage may spend as little as 15 per cent of their time occupied with food. Horses fed ad-lib forage such as hay, haylage or alfalfa (lucerne) do slightly better, but even an average of around 45 per cent of their time spent eating still falls far short of what is ideal for them.

Movement

Horses are built for movement. Although modern populations of feral horses may have little to fear from predators, this was not necessarily so

Above: In the wild, horses travel considerable distances in the course of one day. This group is trekking across part of its home range in the Namib Desert.

for their remoter ancestors. Horses are still prey animals and as such have developed behaviours to deal with possible predators. The most primitive and still the most effective measure is to run away, though horses can and will defend themselves with teeth and hooves if cornered. Nevertheless, running away is their first and best strategy and unless they are trapped they tend not to hang around long enough to get caught. So freedom of movement and the ability to escape when threatened are very important to horses.

In addition, as we have already seen, feral horses move around a great deal. Depending on the local environment, the size of home ranges may vary from just under 1 km^2 (about $\frac{1}{2}$ mile^2) to as much as 48 km^2 (18 $\frac{1}{2}$ miles^2). In the Namib Desert, for example, according to Telané

Right: Horses, especially youngsters like this yearling colt, need the freedom to get rid of excess energy.

Greyling in her 1994 Msc thesis *The behavioural ecology of the feral horses in the Namib Naukluft Park*, the average home range size is 34 km² (13 miles²). But even though horses do not generally cover the whole of their home range within one day, they may traverse a good part of it – eating, moving to better grazing, finding water or sites where they can shelter from the sun or the wind, or where biting insects are less common. In this way they may travel several kilometres a day.

Above: Horses are grazing herbivores who need to eat for around 15 hours out of 24 in order to satisfy their dietary and behavioural needs.

Social interaction

As horses are social animals, social interaction is therefore important to them and it follows that for a horse to remain psychologically healthy it must be allowed access to suitable companions. As foals, feral horses learn how to behave with other horses and how to interact with them in ways that keep social tensions to a minimum. Young stallions learn how to approach and court mares, while the latter learn how to accept the stallion's advances (or to make advances to it) and how to nurture their foals. The latter remain in the security of their family group until the time comes for them to leave the family band. As Chapter 3 will show, horses need some stability in their social lives; constantly having to adjust to new companions can prove extremely stressful for them.

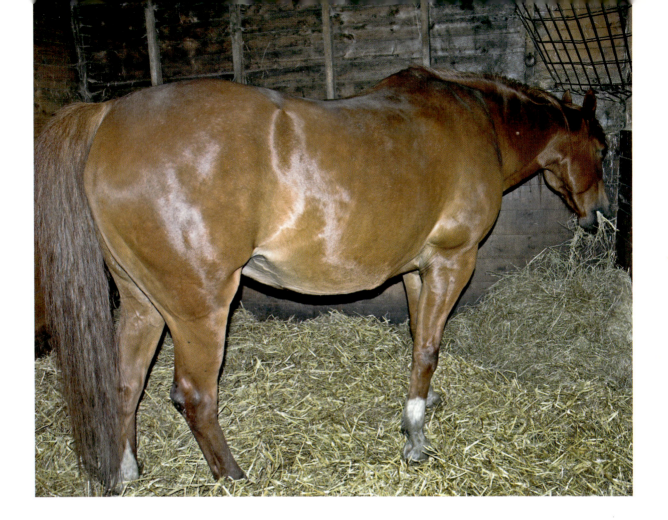

Unfortunately all too many horses are deprived of the opportunity to perform some or all of these natural behaviours. Keeping them confined in stables means that they must eat what they are given, rather than be able to move around to find better food. When their food runs out, they cannot move away to find more. If they drink all their water, or it becomes fouled, they cannot seek a fresh supply. If biting insects attack them in the stable, they cannot move away; they must simply put up with the irritation. And, of course, they are effectively trapped and cannot escape from anything they perceive as danger in their immediate environment.

Many horses competing at a high level are deemed too valuable to risk being turned out with other horses because of the danger of injury. The same horses may be fed a diet rich in cereals but low in forage, which as we have seen greatly restricts the amount of time they spend eating; they may instead spend most of their time simply standing in their stables. If we consider that the only exercise many of these horses receive takes the form of work – and often very intensive work at that – we can see that all too many high-level competition horses are being kept in impoverished environments and prevented from performing behaviours essential to their wellbeing.

However, it is not only competition horses that suffer from an inadequate environment. Many that are kept purely for pleasure are confined in a manner that restricts their opportunity for expressing natural behaviours. This also applies to horses kept for breeding, for although brood-mares and their foals are usually allowed plenty of turnout, they are rarely kept in natural family groups. Foals may be weaned too abruptly and too early, while mares may never have the opportunity to socialize with stallions. The latter may have been segregated from other horses at an early age and never given the opportunity to learn social behaviour with other horses.

All these factors may result in behavioural problems which can be subtle, as in some of the behaviours outlined in Chapter 1, for example lack of co-operation, aggression directed towards other horses or towards humans, irritability, tension, reluctance to go forward under saddle (which may also be a sign of pain), mechanical, zombie-like behaviour and so on. Or the problems may be more severe. For example, they may include hysterical behaviour when separated from companions, rearing or bolting. Both of these are potentially signs of physical as well as psychological distress and pain should always be investigated as a possible cause in these cases or other potentially dangerous behaviour.

Above: Many people worry that horses will injure themselves when they gallop around wildly, as the bay gelding is doing here.

However, some of the most common and among the most disturbing signs that all is not well are the bizarre, apparently meaningless behaviours called stereotypies.

Stereotypies

The term 'stereotypy' is used scientifically to describe a series of fixed, repetitive, obsessive and apparently meaningless behaviour patterns. The disturbed child rocking back and forth, the dog spinning endlessly in circles, the zoo tiger pacing its cage for hours on end – these are all examples of stereotypical behaviour.

Below: This stallion is pacing the fence anxiously because he can see other horses near his equine family and cannot get near to protect them.

One might wonder what an animal gains by such behaviour, since to our eyes it may appear to be meaningless. Over the years many attempts have been made to provide explanations for stereotyped behaviour and what has emerged is that no single explanation is possible as there are many potential causes. Some of the actions may in fact be learned. For

example, if a horse becomes excited when it knows its dinner is about to arrive, it may start to nod its head in anticipation. If the food arrives while it is doing this, its behaviour is being rewarded by the appearance of the food and it is more likely to repeat it. If the food often arrives while it is nodding its head up and down, it may develop into a confirmed head-nodder: in other words its behaviour has been *reinforced* by the arrival of its food, and we would then say that it has been *conditioned* to repeat that behaviour when anticipating its dinner (reinforcement and conditioning are discussed in Chapter 4).

However, it may not repeat the behaviour at any other time, so although this is stereotyped behaviour its performance is restricted to specific times, when the horse is anticipating food, for instance. Horses may display stereotyped behaviour when they are anxious, for example if they are waiting to be let out into the field, or when a mare is temporarily separated from her foal, but again the behaviour may be short-lived and cease as soon as the cause of the anxiety is removed. So it will cease when the horses are let out into the field, or the mare is reunited with her foal. In these situations the horses concerned will usually still respond – even though they may be somewhat distracted – to nearby sights and sounds and to the humans who need to handle them. Other horses, however – and these are the ones giving rise to the greatest concern – may develop stereotypical behaviour that is more than simply a response to a temporary situation. Such horses may spend hours engaged in these fixed, repetitive actions during which time they may be oblivious to anything else that is going on around them.

Horses may display stereotyped behaviour when they are anxious.

Whatever the immediate cause, one thing that has become clear is that stereotypies appear to be a response to a captive environment, since they have not been observed in the wild. The results of research carried out into stereotyped behaviour also suggest that each behaviour pattern has its roots in some form of behaviour that forms part of that animal's natural lifestyle. Hence, the animal appears to be 'acting out' some aspect of that behaviour in an attempt to alleviate frustration at being confined and unable to perform its natural behaviour. For example, the horse confined to the stable may want to leave its stable to run about in the field and get rid of its excess energy, or to socialize with other horses. It cannot get any further than its stable door and so cannot achieve its goal; however that goal is so important to it that it feels the need to make repeated attempts to achieve it, even though it cannot. It therefore 'acts out' the one part of the incomplete behaviour that it *can* perform: it walks towards the door then, unable to get any further, walks away again. This may develop into box-walking (see page 41). Crib-biting (see page 41) appears to have its origins in an attempt to compensate for a diet high in concentrates but low in bulk fibre.

The more we learn about equine behaviour and physiology, the more it becomes clear that horses are creatures with complex brains capable of far more than has generally been believed.

There is some evidence from the studies referred to above that horses may actually become addicted to their stereotype. Unlikely as it may seem, there is a link here to a certain aspect of human behaviour: people who like to run often do so not so much because they want to keep fit (there are other ways of keeping fit that do not involve as much stress on the joints) but because of the 'buzz' it gives them. Studies carried out on stereotypical behaviour suggest that animals that engage in stereotypies involving constant movement may be experiencing a similar 'buzz' to that felt by human runners; this may be what helps to alleviate their distress.

Boredom

One explanation that has often been put forward as a cause of stereotyped behaviour is boredom, but scientists have frequently dismissed this, for two reasons. One is that horses that weave, for example, tend to perform more, not less, stereotyped behaviour when there is a lot of yard activity rather than when the yard is quiet. If the weaving (or whatever stereotypy may be performed) were caused by boredom, one would expect to see less of this behaviour when there is plenty going on for the horse to look at. So boredom cannot be the cause in such instances. The behaviour at such times seems to be triggered instead by a high level of emotional arousal, probably as a result of all the activity going on around the horse. Another reason for dismissing boredom as a cause is that many behavioural scientists have routinely discounted the idea that horses have any kind of mental life – and surely one must have to have such an internal life in order to feel boredom.

However, we should not be too ready to rule out boredom. As we saw in the Introduction, the more we learn about equine behaviour and physiology, the more it becomes clear that horses are creatures with complex brains capable of far more than has generally been believed. We might wonder, though, how an animal that spends the greater part of its day eating, could possibly feel bored. How could horses in the wild keep themselves occupied when they are surrounded by little more than grass? It may be that where food is very scarce horses have to spend so much time finding and consuming food that they do not have much opportunity to amuse themselves in any other way. However, if we watch a group of horses that have unlimited freedom where grasses and shrubs are plentiful, we will see that in the intervals between grazing they find all kinds of things to investigate and play with (including their companions). As Chapter 3 will show, horses not only need social contact, they also need the opportunity for play and relaxation in company.

Individual horses respond in so many different ways to similar situations that one cannot say that those kept in a particular kind of environment will invariably tend to develop stereotypical behaviour. There is some evidence that certain horses are genetically predisposed to develop stereotypies but while such a tendency may appear to run in some families, it may simply be that such families belong to a breed frequently kept in a restricted kind of environment. Examples of such breeds would be Thoroughbred and Arabian racehorses, Arabian show horses, and so on.

Above: Horses are inquisitive. This horse is investigating a piece of black plastic sacking in his stable.

In horses, stereotypies have often been thought of as vices (and in many countries must be declared as such if the animal is sold), as though they were mischievous actions resulting from a bad disposition. Sadly, some people still refer to them like this, even though we now know that they are not vices at all but the horse's attempt to cope with an inadequate lifestyle.

Stereotypical behaviour in horses may take the form of weaving, box-walking, head-nodding, crib-biting, and wind-sucking; in some cases a horse may perform more than one of these behaviours – weaving and crib-biting, for example.

Weaving

The horse stands in its stable and waves its head from side to side. It may also rock from one foot to the other. This is essentially a frustrated movement behaviour: the horse wants to move about freely but because it is confined to a stable it cannot fulfil its need for movement adequately. Weaving appears to have a hypnotic effect on the horse,

Above: Grilles such as this are ineffective in preventing weaving.

which may stand for hours waving its head and/or rocking from side to side.

Many people attempt to 'cure' weavers by fitting an anti-weaving grille with a V-shaped opening, which fits over the stable half-door so that the horse can still look out, but cannot weave its head from side to side. Another popular 'remedy' is to hang two bricks from the doorframe so that if the horse attempts to weave it will hit its head on the bricks. Risk of injury aside, this and the weave grid simply mask the problem. Horses certainly tend to weave at the stable door, but just because it is prevented from weaving in the doorway this does not stop it from weaving further back in the stable! In fact most confirmed weavers will do this if they cannot weave *at* the doorway; this may actually make the problem worse, because the weaver's sense of frustration is increased by its being prevented from looking out over its stable door.

Box-walking

In many ways this is an even more distressing phenomenon than weaving. The horse walks round and round the stable, almost robotically, often keeping this up for hours at a time. Like weaving, this is an attempt on the part of the horse to deal with its frustrated need for movement. Box-walkers will often be poor doers because they are spending the time they should be eating in this travesty of equine movement.

Attempts to prevent box-walking usually involve either tying the horse up or placing obstacles in its way; a favourite 'remedy' is to place a series of car tyres in the stable where the horse normally box-walks. This may work in some cases but box-walkers are notoriously adept at finding ways to avoid the tyres while continuing with their robot-like walking. Furthermore, the obstacles – be they tyres or anything else – may prevent the horse from lying down and obtaining the rest it must surely need very badly.

The horse walks round and round the stable, almost robotically, often keeping this up for hours at a time.

Head-nodding

The horse stands in one place and nods its head up and down repeatedly and for prolonged periods. It may stand still as it does this or it may perform a *piaffe*-like movement (alternately raising one diagonal pair of feet, as in the trot, but remaining in one place). Sometimes the latter consists only of raising alternate forefeet. However, unlike a true *piaffe* this is not a collected movement but a hasty, agitated snatching up of the feet and then setting them down again; the feet may not be actually raised from the ground but simply half-lifted and then put down again.

Crib-biting

The horse takes hold of something (such as the top of its stable half-door, a fixed manger, a fence or the top of a gate) with its incisors (front teeth), arches its neck, pulls back and then lets go abruptly. It may grunt as it does so, although not all crib-biters do this.

Crib-biting is often associated with wood-chewing in general, but not all crib-biters actually chew wood and wood-chewing does not necessarily lead to crib-biting. Owners often attempt to cure crib-biters and wood-chewers by painting their stables with foul-tasting substances to put the horse off.

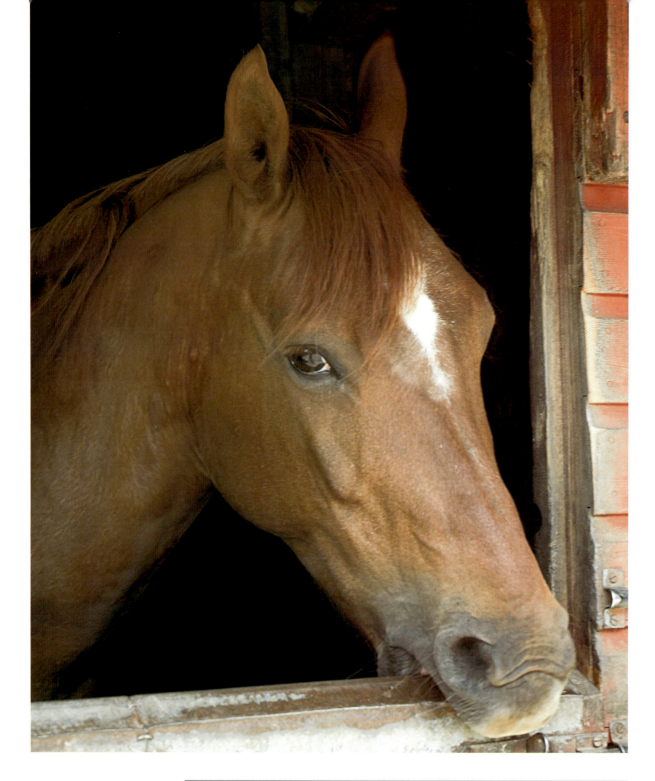

Wind-sucking

Wind-sucking is often confused with crib-biting, possibly because so many crib-biters tend to grunt as they let go of whatever it is they are biting, giving the impression that they are gulping air. However, crib-biting and wind-sucking are not the same thing. True wind-sucking is just that: the horse appears to lick or swallow the air, although recent research suggests that this is not in fact what is happening. It is not clear exactly what the horse is doing and perhaps this will only be understood when further research has been carried out. Whatever is *actually* happening, however, it is certainly bizarre and distressing behaviour and is often seen in horses that also crib-bite. Wind-suckers may have collars fitted to stop them from swallowing air, or even have operations to cut certain muscles in their necks to prevent them from wind-sucking. Both these 'remedies' are also sometimes tried on crib-biters in the mistaken belief that they too are gulping air.

Attempts to cure these stereotypies usually fail because they try to cure the symptoms without addressing the causes. Moreover, preventing a horse from performing its stereotypy is not only ineffective but also detrimental to its welfare since depriving a horse of its only means of coping with its situation does nothing more than exacerbate the problem and may actually cause total breakdown.

Improving the environment

It is always far better to start by improving the environment so that the horse has more opportunity to perform its natural behaviours. If we compare the lifestyles of many horses in domestic settings, it becomes easier to see what aspects of their lifestyle cater to their behavioural needs, and what aspects are lacking in this respect. Looking at the table on page 134 we can see that the ability to perform natural behaviours decreases with the amount of time the horse is confined to its stable and fed limited amounts of forage. Unfortunately, the horse that is confirmed in a stereotypy may well prove impossible to cure, although an improvement in its management could well reduce the behaviour's severity. Milder cases, or those where the stereotypy has not yet become confirmed, are more likely to respond to an improved environment. Longer spells of turnout with compatible companions would be a good start, as would the provision of ad-lib forage for horses that must spend long spells confined to a stable. The latter could also be given an environment enriched by social companionship (such as a neighbour that the horse is able to see and touch), mental challenges such as stable 'toys' which require it to think and work at solving a problem, and so on.

It would be even better if we could change our established management practices so as to prevent behavioural problems related to environment from occurring, or at least minimize the likelihood of their doing so.

Prevention is always preferable to cure!

Wind-suckers may have collars fitted to stop them from swallowing air, or even have operations to cut certain muscles in their necks to prevent them from wind-sucking.

Chapter *3*

The need for companionship and an active social life

Below: This mare and foal are able to relax completely knowing that their stallion is nearby and ready to protect them.

AS WE saw in Chapter 2, horses are social animals and for a prey species, social living brings many benefits, a major one for animals in the wild being safety, because a group is better equipped to deal with predators than a single animal. Apart from safety in numbers, when the group is resting one or two of its members can act as 'lookouts', allowing the others to rest in peace, safe in the knowledge that if danger approaches they will be warned in time to escape.

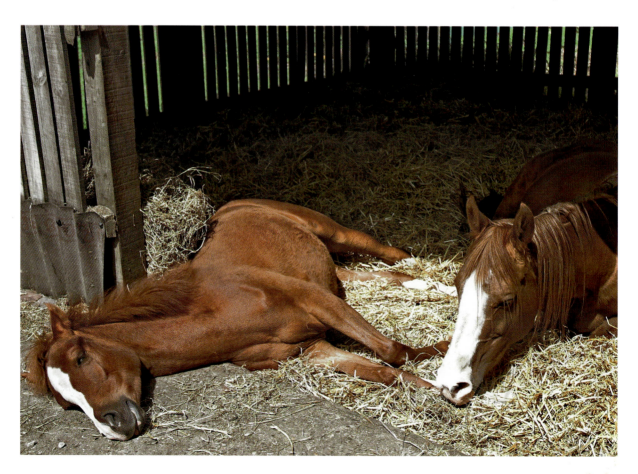

Moreover, some of the equid species, such as zebras, have what is known as disruptive colouration. This is a pattern of markings – in the zebra's case, stripes – that do not follow the contours of the body. It is thought this may make it difficult for predators to distinguish individuals in a group and so target a particular one. The fact that residual striping appears (mainly on the legs) of some modern domestic horses suggests that all horses may once have been more or less striped.

However, there are other benefits to group living: grazing animals need to know where to find food and water, shade from the sun, shelter from bad weather, flies and so on, and as the older members of the group will have such ecological knowledge the younger members will benefit from this. In their turn, they will be able to pass it on to their own offspring.

The family group

As we know, horses are gregarious by nature and have a great need for social interaction with their own kind, preferably in a small, comparatively stable group, and this is how they live in the wild. A family band usually consists of a stallion, or, more rarely, two stallions, plus several mares (generally not more than five) and their offspring. Usually these will be under two years old, although occasionally offspring remain

Above: An equine family consisting of a chestnut mare, a grey stallion and their colt foal.

Above: Foals ideally learn how to approach and interact with other horses within the family group. This youngster is playing with his father, who is extremely tolerant of his son's boisterous play.

with the family band until they are older. In some areas, such as the Namib Desert, a band may consist of as few as two members, although the average elsewhere seems to be between five and seven. This family band may stay together for many years and even after the offspring leave to join a band or form their own, they may still encounter and recognize their family band. Stallions meeting their male offspring after the latter have left the band may greet and play with them.

Restricted social lives

This kind of family group is comparatively rare in domestic settings, although some enlightened breeders do make attempts to allow their breeding stock to form family groups as far as may be practicable. In general, however, the social interactions of domestic horses take place in extremely unnatural circumstances, and in some cases are either severely restricted or even altogether absent.

One of the commonest reasons for restricting horses' social interactions is the belief held by many people that horses are naturally aggressive and if turned out together will inevitably fight. This assumption has been strengthened by scientific studies which have tended to over-emphasize aggressive behaviour (perhaps because it is easier to identify than friendly or neutral behaviour), and by many trainers who have incorporated this emphasis in their training.

Hierarchies and 'pecking orders'

This follows from the common assumption, made by countless trainers, behavioural scientists and ethologists that horses, like many other mammals, organize their social lives according to a dominance hierarchy or 'pecking order' based on aggression. In fact, long-term studies such as those by Joel Berger of the horses of the Granite Range of Nevada, and by Telané Greyling among the horses of the Namib Desert, have shown that dominance is virtually irrelevant in the family lives of these horses. Some behavioural scientists continue to insist it **is** relevant, but they have not given convincing reasons why they believe this.

Below: Mares and stallions need to learn how to socialize with each other in order to interact properly when mating. This chestnut mare and grey stallion are very relaxed with each other.

Above: Horses who belong to a stable group often share food with each other; here an Arabian gelding (right) shares a pile of hay with a yearling colt.

Dominance plays a part only where there is some resource to be competed over and though competition is a significant feature of the social lives of some animals, this is not so for horses. Apart from occasional contests between stallions over access to mares (disputes which take up only a tiny fraction of equine social life), there is virtually nothing for horses to compete over in the wild. Some jostling may occur at waterholes but even then the members of a group are generally very tolerant of each other. Systematic studies have shown that even in times of shortage, competition over food and water is not common among feral horses. Their food is all around them so either there is sufficient for all of them, or all suffer from the shortage. Hence there are few situations in which competition arises among feral horses living in natural family groups. Aggression generally occurs when a horse feels threatened (for instance when another horse invades its personal space, as defined later in this chapter) or when a mare is protecting her foal – when other horses approach a newborn foal too closely, for example.

Leadership

The most dominant or aggressive horse is not necessarily the leader; any horse may take the lead, although not all are followed. The horses most likely to be followed by other horses seem to be those that have the most experience, and this is not because they are dominant, but because they know where to find grazing, shelter, water and so on. The idea that there is one horse that directs the movements of the group is largely a myth. So, although horses may follow an experienced horse, whether it's a mare or a stallion, we should not assume that the horse they are following had any intention of leading them anywhere!

Aggression

Because natural family groups are not common in domestic settings, most people do not have an opportunity to see how horses in such groups behave with each other. They will not see how little aggression there is, or how much friendly interaction occurs. However, aggression is certainly more common in domestic groups of horses because they are often put in situations where they have to compete for some resource.

Below: Stallions who are allowed to interact socially with mares are happier and more relaxed than those who are only ever allowed to cover mares in-hand. Here the grey stallion is courting the chestnut mare prior to mating with her.

This may be personal space, especially in small corrals or paddocks, or when passing through gateways where they may be crowded. Water buckets or troughs may be too small to accommodate all the horses comfortably, or they may be sited in places where horses have to push and shove in order to get near them. In addition, many domestic horses have concentrate feed fed to them out in the field or paddock, and because of the feed's attractiveness to the animals it may increase aggression among a group.

Geldings, like stallions that are kept apart from mares, may never learn how to interact with mares and, if they are subsequently introduced into a mixed group, may react aggressively.

In natural family groups most of the horses will have known each other for years – with the exception of mares recently acquired by the stallion. They have learned how to get on with each other and so social tensions are low. Domestic groups, on the other hand, are usually made up of unrelated horses. In some situations, for example in livery yards or on farms where horses may come and go and are replaced by others as clients leave, or where different horses are acquired by clients or yard owners, they may not have known each other for very long. Social tensions are bound to be higher in such situations as strange horses get to know each other and learn to tolerate each other – or not, as the case may be! Certain horses in such groups may not have been well socialized as youngsters and may have poor social skills. As we shall see later in this chapter, this may be especially so in the case of horses weaned early or abruptly as foals.

Single-sex groups

In addition, horses in domestic settings are often kept in large, single-sex groups. Some people insist that mares and geldings should never be kept together as geldings may be aggressive towards mares. This does sometimes happen but it is seldom a problem in places where mares and geldings are kept together as a matter of course. Problems are much more likely to arise if the sexes are segregated at an early age. Geldings, like stallions that are kept apart from mares, may never learn how to interact with mares and, if they are subsequently introduced into a mixed group, may react aggressively. The same can apply to mares that have been segregated from male horses. Such aggression is not normal in stable (settled) mixed groups where the numbers are kept low. My own research suggests, however, that aggression levels are often much higher in single-sex groups.

Behavioural problems certainly arise where horses are denied the freedom to interact with others of their own kind. We talked in Chapters

1 and 2 about the fact that in many domestic stable yards horses are housed separately and are unable to touch their neighbours. Yet a considerable part of a feral horse's life is devoted to activities that involve close contact with other horses, though the degree of contact varies according to the relationship the horse has with others. Generally speaking, only close friends or family members will be allowed into the horse's most intimate zone of personal space, which is usually between 0 and 2 m (0–6 ½ ft). Nevertheless, this closeness, and the physical contact that does occur, plays an essential role in the horse's social activities.

Above: Close friends may spend a great deal of time in each other's personal space, often grazing side by side like the two horses in this photograph.

Grooming activities and play

Grooming activities are especially important because they relate to physical and mental wellbeing. Horses, like many other social animals, groom each other to get rid of parasites, dirt, loose hair and dead skin. However, there is yet another feature of mutual grooming that underlines its significance to horses. It is a very intimate act, which has the effect of sealing and strengthening social and emotional bonds

Above: Friends can use each other as scratching posts.

between horses. For animals that depend on each other so much in the wild state, this makes mutual grooming an extremely important aspect of equine social life. Although horses have long, reasonably flexible necks, and their spines are capable of bending far more than is generally recognized, they cannot reach certain areas of their bodies to carry out the necessary grooming. So they rely on other horses to take care of those areas for them and, because they are a co-operative species, they respond in kind.

Mutual grooming has another function besides the purely physical aspect: grooming has been shown to reduce the heart-rate of the horse being groomed, so it is an important means of relaxation and release from tension.

Horses will often attempt to groom the human who is brushing their coat; almost everyone who has ever scratched a horse on its neck or withers, for example, will have seen the way its muzzle narrows and elongates, as if it were about to perform the same action on another horse. If you allow the horse to groom you, you may be surprised by how vigorous the action can be; yet it may sometimes be extremely gentle.

Because horses use their teeth to nibble at their equine grooming partner's skin, and because their own skin is much looser and more mobile than a human's, they do not realize that this action can actually be painful for the human. However, people who can endure a little discomfort, and who do not mind their clothes being mistreated, can find that allowing oneself to be groomed by a horse is a wonderful way of bonding with it.

Even the kind of grooming that is carried out solely with the intention of making the horse look good can, if carried out with consideration for the horse, help to relax it and to enhance one's relationship with it. This may be one reason why many horses seem fonder of their grooms than of their riders, where these are not the same person, because the groom not only brings the horse food and water, but also performs this grooming service, which enhances the horse's comfort and sense of wellbeing. One of the most effective methods of grooming involves using the fingers rather than a brush. Because this mimics to some extent the sensation a horse must feel when being groomed by another horse, most horses seem to prefer it to being groomed with a brush. In fact, using the flat of the hand after such a grooming session can bring up a wonderful shine to the coat that is far superior to anything one can achieve with conventional grooming kit.

Below: Mutual grooming is an extremely important part of equine social life.

Studies of feral horses have shown that as much as 10 per cent of their time may be spent in grooming activities and play, and in the case of foals this may be as much as 35 per cent. When one considers that up to 60 per cent of a horse's day consists of grazing, this 10 per cent accounts for a comparatively high proportion of its remaining activities! Observation of my own and other people's horses suggests that the amount of time devoted to grooming and play in free-ranging groups of horses where grazing is plentiful, or in stable domestic groups allowed plenty of turnout time, is comparable to what has been observed among feral horses. Other social behaviours include standing nose-to-tail swishing flies away from each other, or simply loafing, relaxing in the company of other family members or with friends.

Right: Grooming is not just for keeping clean but a way of strengthening social bonds. This can work with the horse-human relationship too.

Below: Horses like to relax by simply loafing in the company of congenial companions.

Social deprivation and behavioural problems

The evident importance of these social activities underlines the degree of deprivation suffered by horses that are not allowed to socialize with others. Some, especially those trained for top level competition, particularly dressage, are never turned out because they are considered too valuable to be allowed to risk injuring themselves, whether through aggressive behaviour, over-excitement leading to galloping around, or from rough play. Some horses are simply never turned out at all, whether with companions or alone, again because their owners fear they will injure themselves in the field. Ironically, it is precisely those horses that are seldom turned out that are most likely to injure themselves through over-excitement.

Horses used to going out every day with the same companions are far less likely to hurt themselves because they will be accustomed to the turnout environment and to other horses and are much less prone to over-react to anything new or exciting. There can never be any guarantee

Below: Foals need to learn how to interact with older horses. This nine-month-old foal, turned out for the first time without his dam, has been 'adopted' by the big bay gelding.

that a horse will not injure itself in the field, but the cost of the alternative – keeping a horse cooped up in a stable – can be very high indeed.

As we saw in Chapter 2, lack of adequate turnout can create stereotypic behaviour in horses. Colic, which can be caused by stress, is a recurring problem for many horses confined to stables, and lack of turnout and companionship can also create other behavioural problems. Horses that are never turned out with other horses may become insecure and over-dependent on the trainer/handler. We can often see this with stallions kept apart from other horses; if they are attached to whoever looks after them they may become distressed and difficult to manage when that person is absent from their lives. Horses whose social contact with other horses is very restricted may develop a similar kind of attachment to one or more equine companions and may become severely distressed and even hysterical when they are separated from those companions.

In some cases, even where horses are turned out with others, there may be little stability within the group because horses are frequently added to the group or removed from it. Some writers have suggested that every time this happens it results in social disruption because the horses in the group have to re-establish their 'pecking order'. As we have seen, however, such 'pecking orders' do not arise in the wild. Rather, they appear to be a response to unnatural conditions, such as when humans create competition by restricting access to water (because, for example, there is only one water bucket or trough in the field), feeding concentrate feed out in the field or corral, confining horses to small areas where they are likely to invade each other's personal space, and so on. Stable groups, where the horses have known each other and lived together for a number of years, are much less likely to suffer social disruptions just because of the temporary removal of one or more of their number.

Horses that are never turned out with other horses may become insecure and over-dependent on the trainer/ handler.

Routine

We are often told that it is essential in horse management to establish and then stick to a set routine for our horses. However, feral and free-ranging horses do not have set routines. Horses are creatures of habit, but what they crave is not a routine as such but settings, people and, above all, other horses that are familiar to them. This, rather than the establishment of 'pecking orders' or hierarchies, is why the removal of horses from an established group, or the introduction of a strange horse, can create social disruptions.

Early weaning

Foals are frequent casualties of management practices that deprive horses of a more natural lifestyle. They are often weaned far too early and too abruptly. As we saw in Chapters 1 and 2, this can create stresses which result in poor health and in some cases may even prove fatal. In the wild, foals would not normally stop suckling until their dam is about to have her next foal, in other words until they are at least a year old. However, many mares do not have a foal every year, and in such cases they may allow the last foal to continue suckling. One of my own homebred horses, that has never been weaned as such, continued to take milk from her dam until she was five years old! Foals (and even yearlings that have not been weaned) can often be seen rushing to take milk whenever they are frightened or have an unsettling experience. This shows that suckling is not only a source of nutrition but also of comfort. However, all too many foals are deprived of this maternal comfort just when they need it most, for instance when they are starting to explore more and learn about the world and all the potentially scary things in it.

Below: Young horses have to learn how to approach and interact with older horses. This yearling colt is approaching his father deferentially.

Many people continue to keep their horses in accordance with management systems more suited to a time when horses worked hard and had to be ready for work at any time of the day.

One result of early and/or abrupt weaning can be to make the horse in question anti-social with its own kind. This is especially true if the horse in question was weaned together with other foals rather than in a mixed-age group. Other foals do not have the necessary social experience to guide them in their relationships with other horses. They have to learn this by trial-and-error, for example by approaching older horses and gauging their reactions and by observing how other horses relate to each other. If they are separated from their dams and kept in a same-age group before they have begun to socialize properly, they will not learn how to approach and interact with older horses. The other foals with which they are weaned will not have this experience either, so there is no one from which they can learn the art of social interaction. When they are finally put into a mixed-age group, they may be socially inept and as a result suffer all kinds of rebuffs. If they have been made to feel insecure by being abruptly separated from their dams, they may not know how to react to these rebuffs and as a result their insecurity can render them incapable of making or accepting friendly overtures to other horses.

It would be much better – and I have certainly found this to be the case – to separate foals gradually from their dams when they are approximately nine months to a year old. This can be done by putting them for short spells in separate fields or paddocks where they can still see each other, ensuring that the foal is with adult horses that it knows and with which it feels safe. The periods of separation can be extended and the foal gradually moved out of sight of its dam, until they will tolerate being separated for prolonged periods without becoming stressed. This may take more time and effort but is surely preferable to the avoidable distress that must otherwise ensue.

Inappropriate management

As with so much that happens in the horse world, management systems tend to be based mainly on what has gone before, regardless of whether such systems are still appropriate, let alone actually work to the horse's advantage. Many people continue to keep their horses in accordance with management systems more suited to a time when horses worked hard and had to be ready for work at any time of the day, and so it was not practical to let them spend time out at grass with other horses.

Ironically, many horses may have been far better off socially in the days when they were used in warfare. Although they worked hard and risked death or injury in battle, cavalry horses on campaign were constantly in

the company of their own kind. They were tethered alongside each other, ate and drank together, and shared all the hardships of the campaign together. They were seldom isolated as so many horses are nowadays.

I do believe that most horse owners want to do their best for their horses, but are hampered by the influences of equestrian cultures geared to *our* convenience rather than the comfort and wellbeing of horses. Ironically, however, management systems that result in horses being kept stabled for considerable periods of time are actually very labour-intensive because horses kept in must not only be groomed and fed, their stables must also be mucked out. Yet people who do not relish the idea of grooming a horse that is muddy or dusty because it has been out in the field or paddock will happily spend hours performing all the stable chores that come with a stabled horse!

The horse that spends as much time as possible turned out with familiar, compatible companions may not be as immaculate as the stabled horse (although horses can keep each other's coats extremely well groomed and shiny!) but it will be happier, healthier and more relaxed. Moreover, because its physical and psychological needs are being satisfied, it will be much more receptive to the idea of co-operating with humans. This would surely make life easier and more pleasant for all concerned!

Above: Horses housed in separate stables cannot sniff at or touch each other and so are deprived of an important part of social interaction.

Chapter *4*

Training: principles versus methods

F EW OTHER domestic animals – except perhaps the various breeds of working dog – have been asked to work for humans in such a variety of ways as horses. In the past they were used for war, farm work and transport, and in some areas of the world are still used for the last two – and comparatively recently were still used in conflict situations. In addition, horses are a vital component in certain law-enforcement agencies in various parts of the world. And of course, in the modern western world they take part in a variety of competitive disciplines as well as being kept purely for leisure activities such as hacking out and trekking.

Regardless of the purpose for which the horse is kept, training is obviously essential.

Purpose of training

Regardless of the purpose for which the horse is kept, training is obviously essential, or we will not get very far at all. Training can be carried out for the purpose of suppling and strengthening the horse in order to school it for ridden work and to prepare it for whatever equestrian disciplines in which it is to take part. We could call this *athletic* training. Training can also be carried out in order to make the horse manageable so that it can be handled with ease and its physical needs attended to. We can call this *behavioural* training. Athletic and behavioural training can overlap, as we shall see in this chapter and the next.

Different methods

Nowadays, a huge number of different behavioural training methods are being promoted, with many of them being given impressive sounding names accompanied by jargon that often obscures what is actually going on when these methods are applied. This can be very confusing for horse owners wanting to do the best for their charges but unsure about which

Above: Athletic training is carried out for the purpose of suppling and strengthening the horse for ridden work.

Left: Schooling over jumps can be beneficial in athletic training.

Above: Much of behavioural training is aimed at making the horse more manageable. Charles Wilson works here with Kieros (Anglo-Arab x Lusitano gelding).

direction to take. Yet once we cut through the jargon we can see that regardless of what method is being promoted, or what label we choose to give that method, all behavioural (and some athletic) training is based on the same basic principles: the learning principles known as *conditioning*. It is important that we recognize this, because failure to understand the process of training can get us into terrible trouble.

Conditioning

The great thing about conditioning is that it works with any animal capable of learning, regardless of species – and that includes us too. Knowing how conditioning works can help us to understand the cause of a great many behavioural problems, find ways to deal with them and, one hopes, prevent many of them from arising in the first place.

Classical conditioning

There are two types of conditioning. One of these, known as *classical* or *Pavlovian* conditioning, builds on reflexes. For example, in his now famous experiments on dogs, the Russian scientist Ivan Pavlov found that

Above: Charles Wilson moves Kieros around using clear signals via body language.

they salivated when meat powder was put on their tongues (a reflex response). By ringing a bell at the same time as the meat powder was placed on the tongues, and repeating this action a number of times, Pavlov was then able to produce the salivation reflex simply by ringing the bell – without the use of the meat powder at all. This is called a *conditioned response*. Suppose a horse is being ridden past a certain tree when someone fires a gun, making the horse jump in fright (a reflex response). Every time it passes the same tree after that, it starts in fright, even though no gun has been fired. The fright reflex has become a conditioned response to passing that tree, although the tree itself had nothing to do with the original fright – it just happens to be what the horse noticed when it had the fright. So we can see how easily such an experience can lead to what we perceive as a behavioural problem.

We can help horses to overcome fears created by situations like this, as well as take steps to prevent fears from taking hold, by a process called *habituation*. The horse is gradually (with the emphasis on *gradually*) accustomed to a potentially scary stimulus. An example of this is given in Chapter 7, where I describe ways of accustoming horses to loading and travelling in horseboxes and trailers.

Operant conditioning

The other type of conditioning is called *operant* conditioning, which is based around *consequences*. The subject performs a behaviour (that is, it *operates* within the environment), often in response to a cue or *stimulus*, which has a certain consequence, and the nature of the consequence (otherwise called a *reinforcer*) increases the probability that the subject will repeat the behaviour that led to the consequence. For example, suppose we want a horse to take a step back. Once way of asking it to do this is to put pressure on the headcollar in a backward direction – towards its rear. If it steps back in response to this, we ease off the pressure – or we should! If we repeat this a few times, the horse quickly learns that all it has to do to be free of the pressure of the headcollar on its nose and poll is to step back. So the behaviour of stepping back has been reinforced by the fact that we remove the pressure. Of course, the effectiveness of this depends on the degree to which the horse minds the pressure on its nose and poll!

Below: Backward pressure on the headcollar encourages the horse to step back in order to release pressure, which must be removed the instant he complies.

So in this example the stimulus = pressure » consequence (behaviour) = horse steps back » pressure ceases (reinforcer) = increases likelihood that next time someone puts backward pressure on the headcollar it will step back. A reinforcer is therefore something that increases the tendency of a human or non-human animal to repeat an action or behaviour. Misunderstandings regarding the different kinds of reinforcement are very common. Many people confuse *negative* reinforcement with punishment, and even some very experienced trainers fail to understand the difference. It is important that we clear up these misunderstandings as they can lead us down the wrong track and obscure what is really going on.

Negative reinforcement is **not** the same as punishment, and to avoid confusion and misuse of training principles we need to know just what negative reinforcement is.

Suppose you are in a crowd of people with a friend who knows in which direction you need to go, but you do not. There is a lot of noise and you cannot hear what the friend is saying when she tells you to turn left. So she puts her hand on your shoulder and gently steers you in the direction you need to go. You do not want to resist the pressure of your friend's hand, so you turn away from the pressure. The instant you start to move in the right direction, the friend removes her hand. When the pressure is removed, that reinforces the turn (if she kept on pressing, you might get annoyed, because you would not know where she wanted you to go and might even end up going round in circles). Without even thinking about it too much, you have moved in the right direction. That is an example of negative reinforcement; the word negative refers to the fact that the reinforcement consists of taking something away. In this instance the thing to be avoided is the pressure of your friend's hand – and note that this does not have to be something unpleasant, although it could be if your friend used too much pressure; when it is removed, that is the reinforcer.

A stimulus or cue such as the pressure referred to above is often referred to as an *aversive* stimulus. In behaviour modification terms, this refers to something the subject wants to avoid. This is unfortunate, because it immediately conjures up something unpleasant, whereas an aversive stimulus might actually be something very mild, as in the example just given. I think that for this reason it is not a good description, although scientifically it may be an accurate one, and so I will use the term stimulus (or cue, if it's more appropriate) on its own.

We can see from this that much of what we do with horses consists of negative reinforcement. The horse moves away from the pressure of the rider's leg, yields to the pressure of the bit, or steps sideways in order to re-balance itself in response to a change in the rider's weight distribution. In good riding this use of negative reinforcement will be as mild as possible and used in conjunction with frequent rewards.

Rewards

So what counts as a reward? The removal of a stimulus or the cessation of a cue is often referred to as a *reward*, without any further explanation. Say the handler asks the horse to walk forward by pulling on the lead rope and then easing off as the horse advances. The release of pressure when the horse complies may be described as a reward. In fact it is negative reinforcement because it consists of taking something away (removing the pressure when the horse walks forward). To take another, exaggerated example: suppose someone started hitting you and said, 'If

The horse moves away from the pressure of the rider's leg, yields to the pressure of the bit, or steps sideways in order to re-balance itself in response to a change in the rider's weight distribution.

Above: This stallion is receiving his reward for doing as his trainer asked. This is not a bribe but an incentive to co-operate willingly.

you do "X" I'll stop hitting you!' I imagine that for most people things would have to be pretty bad before they would regard relief from being hit as any kind of reward. Yet we could describe this, and the previous example, as negative rewards and we would technically be correct. However, the use of the term 'reward' in this context can be misleading because it implies something pleasant, whereas, as we have just seen, it need not be anything of the kind. It is very easy, when thinking in terms of negative rewards, to overlook the fact that although they are certainly very effective as reinforcers (if they were not, negative reinforcement would not work – and it plainly does) they are not necessarily the best way of motivating a horse, or a human for that matter! The human or non-human whose behaviour results only in negative rewards may end up doing just enough to ensure removal of the pressure, or whatever other stimulus or cue is being employed, and no more. There is no incentive to work any harder than that. For most of us, the notion of a reward implies something *positive*, in other words something added to increase the likelihood of the subject, in this case, a horse, repeating the action that earned them the reward.

Positive reinforcement

This brings us to **positive reinforcement**, which implies some kind of positive reward, in other words, the addition of something pleasant or desirable in order to increase motivation. The reinforcer here is something the subject likes and wants; in the case of a horse this might be a mint, a piece of carrot or other food treat, a stroke, or a scratch on the neck or withers, or indeed whatever the individual horse likes. Suppose you want to catch a horse in the field. If you have a good relationship, and provided it has had no bad experiences that could make the idea of being caught unattractive, it will most probably amble over to you out of curiosity. If you say its name and at the same time give it a reward when it reaches you, it will begin to associate its name with the reinforcer; after a few repetitions it will come when its name is called because it knows the end result will be something pleasant. You have just reinforced its behaviour of coming to you by using positive reinforcement, and its name has become the stimulus or *cue* for it to come to you. Once this behaviour is established and the horse comes to you every time, you do not need to reinforce it on every occasion. In fact, it is better if you only use the reinforcer every so often. This is called a *variable schedule of reinforcement* as it keeps the behaviour 'alive' and makes it much more likely that the horse will continue to respond to you calling its name.

Research has shown that although negative reinforcement can be a very effective tool, it is nowhere near as effective as positive reinforcement. The latter is not only more fun for both the subject and trainer, it is streets ahead of negative reinforcement in terms of increasing motivation!

Below: This foal's training has commenced with positive reinforcement: she is learning that humans can be pleasant to be around.

A surprising number of people object to the idea of positive rewards, for reasons that are often obscure. They may believe, or have been taught, that since horses do not give each other presents, the giving of a reward is somehow 'unnatural'. Or they may believe that giving horses food rewards leads to nipping and/or pushy horses. Whatever the reason, such perceptions are based on several misunderstandings. First of all, horses don't give each other 'presents' as such, but they undoubtedly understand and appreciate being given something they find pleasurable. Second, if food rewards are given only in specific circumstances, for example, as a reward for the horse doing what it has been asked, or at specific times, for instance when saying good night, they are unlikely to result in problems. The riders of the Spanish Riding School in

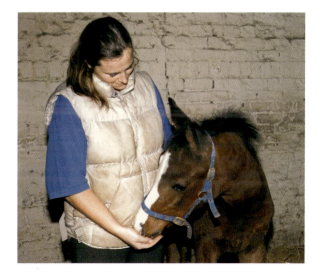

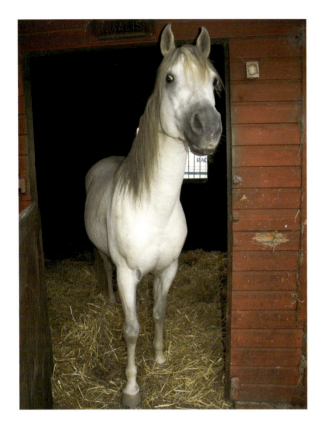

Vienna have been giving the school's Lipizzaner stallions sugar lumps for generations without any adverse effects!

Another objection often put forward is that rewards are a kind of bribe. So is a salary or wage paid to a human a bribe, or is it a just reward for work performed? Let's face it, apart from voluntary work, most people would not work for nothing, no matter how much they liked their boss. Why then should we expect horses to do so? If we do, this assumes that the horse should do things for us because we want it to, rather than because it gets a reward, and indeed this is the basis of many of the training methods known collectively as 'natural horsemanship'. We will look at this in the next chapter; for now we will go on to look at some other aspects of conditioning, such as the different types of *punishment*.

Above: This stallion, who has been trained using positive reinforcement, can be asked to stand in his stable and will not move until told to do so, even when, as here, the stable door is open.

Right: Positive reinforcement can be used to teach horses virtually anything of which they are physically capable. This stallion started to offer this behaviour spontaneously by pawing at the bale of straw; this behaviour was built up by the shaping process referred to in this chapter.

Punishment

Punishment is often confused with negative reinforcement, but as I said earlier, they are not the same thing. In fact they could be said to be opposites, because negative reinforcement acts to *increase* the likelihood of behaviour being repeated, whereas punishment (in theory at least) acts to *decrease* its likelihood. We can either introduce something unpleasant as a punisher (*positive* punishment) or we can deprive the subject of something he or she likes (*negative* punishment).

Many people believe in punishment-based training, either because it is what they have been taught, or because they believe the use of punishment is an effective way to train animals. However, punishment is not really a very good training method. We can use it to tell a subject what *not* to do, but we cannot convey by this means what we want them *to* do. Even if we use it just to get rid of an unwanted behaviour, that behaviour may simply be replaced by another, equally unwanted behaviour; the punishment will do nothing to motivate the subject to switch to the kind of behaviour we do want. In terms of motivation, punishment is therefore rather a hit-and-miss affair. It must be administered immediately and be sufficiently strong to act as a deterrent. The degree of punishment has to be greater than the animal's desire or need to do whatever he is being punished for; or, as with excessive negative reinforcement, the subject may do as we wish, but make only sufficient effort to avoid punishment or the stimulus. Or he may simply make greater efforts to avoid being caught!

People often use punishment illogically. One often sees a rider giving their horse a smack with a whip because it has refused a fence. Such riders will often justify their actions on the grounds that the horse was being naughty in refusing, and they want to 'teach it a lesson'. Quite apart from the fact that the horse might have refused because it was afraid of the jump or unsure whether it could tackle it, how is it supposed to know that its refusal was the reason for its punishment? And how can it know that in order to avoid punishment next time, it had better jump any fence at which its rider points it?

Another common scenario is that in which a rider will punish the horse for some misdeed when it is back in the stable. This is even more illogical than the rider hitting the horse for refusing a jump. How can the horse possibly know what it is being punished for? The same objection applies when people deprive a horse of its dinner because it has been 'naughty'.

Many people believe in punishment-based training, either because it is what they have been taught, or because they believe the use of punishment is an effective way to train animals.

Many people justify such actions on the grounds that 'it worked because the horse never did it again.' How do they know it would have done it (whatever 'it' was) again anyway?

Behaviour analyst Murray Sidman has written at length about the damaging side effects of coercion and punishment, which extend far beyond the circumstances in which they are used. However, this does not mean that we must never use punishment. There may be situations – for example if a horse is behaving aggressively and we do not have enough information to know what is causing the aggression – where we need to take action in order to avoid injury. As Dr Sidman points out in *Coercion and its Fallout* (Authors Cooperative Inc, 2000), in such situations '...common sense tells us that we have to use whatever effective means are at hand.' But as he goes on to say, the occasional emergency 'may justify punishment as a treatment of last resort, but never as the treatment of choice. To use punishment occasionally as an act of desperation is not the same as advocating the use of punishment as a principle of behaviour management.'

Punishment is not – and cannot be – a reinforcer. It is aimed at preventing an unwanted behaviour and so does not reinforce anything; you cannot reinforce behaviour that has not yet occurred! Punishment must therefore **never** be confused with negative reinforcement.

Extinction

So what can we do instead of punishing a horse for unwanted behaviour? One solution that works very well is simply to ignore the behaviour – though obviously this does not apply if it has become dangerous. In such cases behaviour modification is best left to people experienced in the use of positive reinforcement in dealing with dangerous behaviour. Much bad behaviour is part of a bid for attention; one of the commonest examples of this is the colt that nips. It discovers that nipping leads to a reaction from its human handlers, so it nips even more. Attempts to punish it for doing so are unlikely to be successful unless the punishment is extremely severe, and though this may have the desired effect it could also make the colt afraid of humans. It is really much more effective to ignore the nipping (I have found that a thick, padded jacket enables me to do this safely) and reward the colt when it is being good. Because the nipping is not being reinforced it has not resulted in what the colt wants – and it will eventually stop nipping, because there is nothing in it for him, whereas good behaviour results in something pleasant for him. This

Much bad behaviour is part of a bid for attention; one of the commonest examples of this is the colt that nips.

process is called *extinction* and it is a very effective way of getting rid of unwanted behaviour.

Clicker-training

Now that more people are becoming aware of the power of positive reinforcement, *clicker-training* is becoming increasingly popular. It was devised as a way of communicating to animals such as killer whales and dolphins that they have done what the trainer wants. Because the trainer often has to work at a distance from these animals, he or she cannot always let them know the instant they have got something right. By pairing the sound of the clicker (see illustration on page 72) with a positive reinforcer the gap between the behaviour and the reinforcer is closed, as the clicker 'marks' the correct behaviour and tells the animal that something pleasant will be forthcoming.

Some trainers have objected that the clicker encourages a rather 'mechanical' approach in which the trainer feels no need to become emotionally involved with the subject. They feel the training may be reduced to a rather mindless process of stimulus and response. This can certainly happen, and I can sympathize with such concerns. However,

Above: Colts can be very mouthy; this is part of a colt's natural behavioural repertoire, so punishment will not be understood and may make the colt afraid of humans. The best response is to ignore the behaviour, as shown above. Eventually the nipping stopped as it was not being reinforced in any way.

Above: The clicker is a small box containing a metal strip which when pressed makes a clicking noise. This can be used to tell an animal the exact point at which it has done what the human wanted.

when used correctly the clicker can be a far more accurate marker than the trainer's voice. Because the click is instantaneous it can pinpoint the precise moment when the animal's action is correct. Say, for example, you are lunging a young horse and it goes to canter when you want it to. You can mark this by saying 'Good boy', or just 'Good' or whatever words you want to use. The problem is that by the time you have said the whole word or words the moment may have passed, so although the horse may know in general terms that it has done something right, it won't necessarily know that this was at the exact moment it struck off into canter. This is where the clicker is really useful, especially for people who talk to their horses a lot and who may not realize when they are using words out of the context of training. For example, a lot of people who say 'Good boy' or 'Good girl' when their horse has done well in training also use this phrase in other contexts, and this confuses the horse.

Correct timing

Whatever type of reinforcement we use, it must occur **at the same time** as the action or behaviour being reinforced, or the horse will not make the connection between the action and the reinforcer. You might end up reinforcing the wrong thing, and indeed this is a common cause of unwanted behaviours. For example, suppose you want your horse to move forward. You ask it to move, and it does so. Then, when it has halted again, several seconds later, you give it a piece of carrot.

So what are you actually reinforcing here? You *think* you are reinforcing its movement forward, but in fact you have reinforced standing still, because that was what it was doing when you gave it the carrot! From a simple example like this, we can see how easy it is to train our horses to do the opposite of what we want – quite by accident!

Opposite: This colt had a bad experience with a headcollar just as he was beginning to accept it nicely. This required extensive retraining, starting with getting him to accept the headcollar near his muzzle. Only positive reinforcement was used.

This is not because horses are stupid; on the contrary, many horses are very clever indeed – at being horses! They have no means of knowing exactly what we want them to do; even humans being given instructions in a foreign language that they do not understand would find it difficult to work out what they were being asked to do without being given some clue by the instructor's behaviour.

Shaping

This means that we have to break training down into small steps – sometimes very tiny steps indeed. The moment the horse gives us even a slight approximation of the behaviour or movement we want, we reinforce its action – preferably by using positive reinforcement. Once it is responding reliably, we only reinforce an even closer approximation to what we want, until we have built up the complete behaviour or action. This is called shaping and it is the basis of a great deal that we teach horses.

These are the most basic aspects of conditioning and learning theory. However, in order to understand them fully we need to learn about them in much greater detail than is possible in a book of this nature, and to help you in this, the recommended reading section on page 139 has some suggestions on how to find out more about these principles. There are many very fine trainers working with horses who have never heard of these principles, yet they still manage to put them into practice without ever realizing that this is what they are doing. This means that they can obtain some wonderful results, but all too often when they try to teach others about what they are doing, they end up passing on information about what they *think* they are doing rather than what is *really* happening. This can lead to great discrepancies between what trainers say they do and what they actually do. It can also result in claims being made about the virtues of 'new' training methods versus older, more 'traditional' methods, when in fact there may be no more than a superficial difference between different approaches.

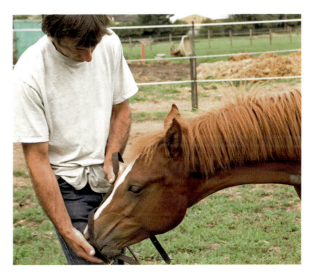

In the next chapter we will look at a 'traditional' approach to training horses under saddle, and take a critical view of so-called 'natural horsemanship'. Is the latter really a revolutionary approach to training horses, or is it a case of 'the more things change, the more they remain the same'?

Chapter 5

How horses respond

Once we understand the training principles outlined in the last chapter, we should be able to see how the various training methods, whatever they are called, apply these principles. We might think that this knowledge would be sufficient, but unfortunately things are not quite as straightforward as that – because if we focus too narrowly on stimuli, conditioning and reinforcement schedules, we are in danger of forgetting that the horse does not merely respond mechanically. It has a brain, which is far more complex than many people realize, and it also has emotions that may get in the way of the

Below: How the leg aids influence the horse.

If the leg is used too far back it will stimulate muscles which support the lumbar spine rather than the part of the spine which lies beneath the rider's seat. This may tip the horse onto his forehand as the back muscles which help to support the forehand are not being brought into action.

Use of the leg here may encourage the horse to extend the forelimbs but this should not be overdone as it does nothing to support the horse's back.

When the rider's leg is in the correct position, the leg aid produces a reflex response in the abdominal muscles, which lifts the horse's back under the rider, giving support to the horse's spine and allowing the hind legs to step under the horse's body. This in turn helps to raise the forehand.

Above: Natural horsemanship: controlling the horse's movements from the ground.

learning process if the training process becomes too pressurized and demanding. And, finally, it has a body capable of responding to physical, auditory and visual stimuli in ways that range from the subtlest of muscle contractions to an explosion of energy and movement. So, understanding the theory of learning is not enough; we must also understand *how* and *why* the horse responds in ways that are specific to it.

The 'natural' approach

The recent explosion of interest in the methods of training known collectively as 'natural horsemanship' (or by some people as 'horse whispering', after the original 'horse whisperer', Dan Sullivan) has created a perceived gulf between those who adopt the 'natural' approach and those who stand by a more 'traditional' approach.

For many people, part of the appeal of so-called 'natural' training methods lies in the 'feel-good' factor resulting from the idea that in using these methods one is working to gain the horse's respect without the use of force. This is perceived to run counter to 'traditional' training methods that supposedly involve a greater or lesser degree of coercion. However, in this context 'traditional' may mean anything one wants it to, since the form equestrian traditions take will depend a great deal on the local culture. The ironic thing is that very often the methods promoted by natural horsemanship trainers use the same kind of principles as the traditional methods they are rejecting! Often this is not apparent because the methods are supposed to be based on the horse's natural behaviour, but the problem is that many trainers rely on faulty assumptions and inadequate knowledge.

Many people might think that it hardly matters whether these assumptions are correct or not, as long as the methods work. But it does matter, because – as we shall see – this can lead to a discrepancy between what trainers say they are doing and what is actually happening.

To complicate matters further, there are many trainers working outside the concept of 'natural horsemanship' who have studied learning theory, and seek to incorporate its principles into conventional training,

Below: Sensitive horses, such as this mare and gelding are extremely responsive to the slightest movement on the part of the rider. (Don Francisco de Bragança riding Lusitano mare Queijada and Sylvia Loch riding Lusitano x TB gelding Espada.)

including, of course, training under saddle. Here, too, there is a gulf between what trainers perceive is happening and the reality.

So what is going on in these very different approaches to training horses? I want to start by looking at what happens when we sit on the horse as opposed to working with it from the ground.

Training principles and riding

We can easily see how the training principles already discussed apply in situations in which we want to influence a horse's behaviour. But how do these principles affect what we do with the ridden horse? Can we use them in the same way, or is there something else going on here? And if so, how does it affect the way horses respond to us?

Many modern trainers who have studied the principles of learning theory and conditioning tend to talk as if training a horse were virtually the same as training a dog, and in theory they are correct – up to a point: all mammals, including humans, learn in much the same ways. However, in practice there are some important differences. For example, we can train dogs without even having to touch them, using only positive reinforcement, building on (shaping) spontaneous actions freely offered by the dog. To some degree we can extend this approach to young horses; I have taught foals, for example, to stand, come when called and, among other things, step back – also without laying a finger on them except to give a small amount of food, a scratch or a stroke by way of positive reinforcement. But once we start to train the horse under saddle, we introduce another dimension: if we want to ride it we have no choice but to introduce physical contact into the training process.

We have already seen that much of what we do with horses involves negative reinforcement and although this is very effective, it can easily be used in a severe and oppressive manner. Should this be the case, it is not only unpleasant for the horse but creates a degree of stress, which adversely affects the learning process as well as the animal's general welfare.

For this reason, many thoughtful people insist that they do not use negative reinforcement when riding. Instead they use positive reinforcement to shape the horse's response under saddle, by breaking each movement down into steps and reinforcing each approximation of what they want to achieve. It is theoretically possible to do this but in

I have taught foals, for example, to stand, come when called and, among other things, step back – without laying a finger on them.

practice the very act of sitting on a horse's back is a form of negative reinforcement, as it cannot help but respond in some way to the rider's presence. As one of the great horsemen of the 20th century, Waldemar Seunig, remarks in *Horsemanship* (Allen Classic Series, J.A. Allen 2003, translated from the original German by Leonard Mins), 'Every shift of weight, produced by a deliberate or unintentional movement of the rider, finds a desired or undesired "echo" in the well-tuned instrument of the horse's body.' In the same passage, Seunig goes on to say that he had ridden Lipizzaner stallions at the Spanish Riding School in Vienna that were so sensitive that a change in balance created by the rider inclining his head to one side was enough to make the horse depart from a walk to a gallop towards that side. Of course Seunig was talking about very responsive and highly trained horses, but even the least sensitive of horses cannot avoid reacting in some way to the presence of the rider in the saddle. If that presence is creating discomfort, then whatever action the horse takes to ease that discomfort will be reinforced if it has the desired effect. Or, if the horse feels even slightly unbalanced by the rider, it will move so as to regain its balance. If it succeeds, again its action will have been reinforced. As this is none other than negative reinforcement, the only way we can avoid it altogether is by not getting on the horse at all!

Below: This Arab stallion is very partial to mints. Here he is being given a mint or two after some excellent ridden work.

The rider uses subtle changes of weight distribution as well as slight changes in muscle tone to 'talk' to the horse, who responds by making changes to his own balance and muscle tone.

By touching the horse with the leg in specific places, the rider is able to stimulate the muscles which raise the back, as well as those which facilitate forward movement.

The rider's thigh and knee should be held firmly against the saddle in order to stabilize the seat; however, gripping with the knee blocks the nerve impulses which trigger forward movement. This blocking action helps to halt the horse.

We can certainly make use of positive reinforcement in many ways when riding. We could, for example, mark a good transition, a good square halt, a prompt response, or indeed anything we feel the horse has done well, by saying 'Good!' or 'Good boy', and simultaneously giving it a stroke or a pat (most horses prefer the former) or whatever we have established as being pleasing to the horse. We can even stop and give it a treat; a rest from work is always welcome, especially if it is accompanied by something the horse likes (the horse in the photograph on page 78 is extremely partial to mints).

Above: The rider's position as an aid.

Effective riding

Although we cannot really avoid it if we want to be truly effective riders, the use of negative reinforcement does not have to be unpleasant for the horse. It can consist of the softest and subtlest of touches with the leg, the merest whisper down the reins, the briefest bracing of the rider's abdominal muscles. The horse will respond to all of these aids, which help it understand what the rider wants, if it is given the chance.

Above: Riders need to pay great attention to their position in the saddle. One of the best ways to do this is on the lunge.

Effective riders know how to use their bodies in ways that *help* the horse to respond by making use of its natural reflexes; that is, they make a subtle use of their legs in places where stimulation of the underlying nerves and muscles helps to raise the horse's back (enabling it to carry a rider more efficiently) and move the hind legs forward. Or they influence the horse to make changes of direction, bend, halt and so on by an equally subtle use of their weight in the saddle, together with the influence of the legs. For a fuller understanding of how these aids work, see *The Anatomy of Riding* by Sara Wyche (Crowood Press 2004). Incidentally, the original word for aids was *helps*, from the French *aider*, meaning to help or assist.

However, if we approach riding from the point of view of breaking everything down into tiny steps that can be reinforced, without taking into account the horse-rider interaction, we have missed the point, and the horse may suffer for it. No matter how much positive reinforcement we may use, if the rider hampers the horse by poor balance and posture, then the horse will suffer physically, because its efforts to protect itself from the unbalancing effect of the rider will cause tension, leading ultimately to strain. There is a mental toll as well, because while the horse's brain is telling it to respond its body is preventing it from doing so correctly.

Misuse of reinforcement

Riders and trainers often use the principles of reinforcement (whether knowingly or otherwise) in an effort to 'teach' the horse to respond in certain ways. Take, for example, the horse that hollows its back and raises its head because the rider is sitting badly. These are reflex actions over which the horse has little control as the weight on its back stimulates such reflexes. The proper solution would be for the rider to sit correctly. However, in an attempt to teach the horse how to carry its head and neck (as if it did not know how to be a horse!), it may be put into draw-reins. Because of the strain this places on the ligaments of the neck and back, the result is often long-term damage to those ligaments, as well as giving the horse a headache. Yet all too often the horse is blamed for not learning how to carry itself better and the rider says 'He should know better by now!' or 'He's just trying it on'.

Below: Draw reins are frequently used, especially before competitions. However they should only be used by people who understand exactly how they work and whether they are actually appropriate to a particular horse.

The horse looks superficially impressive, but his outline is hollow and his hind legs are not working efficiently; he is actually being pulled along by his forehand. This would not be so important if he did not have to carry the burden of the rider. In order to avoid strain the horse must be able to raise the centre of his back. If the horse is hampered by the rider then no amount of conditioning will be able to 'teach' him to carry himself properly in a way that minimizes strain and injury to his back and limbs.

Although the horse's head and neck are raised, this is a false head carriage. Because the rider's position is 'locking up' his back muscles, the horse is obliged to use the muscles on the underside of his neck to prop up his forehand.

Because she is unbalanced, the rider cannot take responsibility for her own weight, which acts to 'lock up' the horse's long back muscles. This in turn prevents him from using his hind legs to carry himself properly; he is effectively 'strung out' behind instead of being 'together'. The hind leg stride is therefore restricted.

Above: How an unbalanced rider can affect a horse.

It is certainly far better to understand the principles of reinforcement than to remain in ignorance of them, but until riders and trainers alike also understand how the horse's anatomy dictates what, how and when we train it, learning theory on its own is like the proverbial 'razor in the hands of a monkey.'

The classical approach

The great masters of equitation, whose teachings form part of the equestrian body of knowledge that is often termed 'classical', understood how the structure of the horse's anatomy affects what we ask of it, and how it reacts to the rider who knows how to evoke the sensory responses referred to earlier in this chapter. They worked from Xenophon's principle that anything forced can never be beautiful, as set out in his quote from an earlier master, Simon of Athens (c.400BC): 'For what the horse does under compulsion...is done without understanding; and there is no beauty in it either, any more than if one should whip and spur a dancer. There would be a great deal more ungracefulness than beauty in either a horse or a man that was so treated'.

This piece of wisdom, from Xenophon's *Peri hippikes* (translated by M.H. Morgan as *The Art of Horsemanship*, J.A. Allen 1962) is no less relevant

now than it was when it was set down by Xenophon (c.444–c.357BC) around 360BC.

When the horse moves freely under saddle, performing willingly and without constraint, and when horse and rider form a harmonious partnership, the result may be said to be truly classical. Interestingly, its practitioners often refer to this classical approach as 'working in harmony with nature'. This is precisely the claim made by adherents of 'natural horsemanship'. So how natural is the latter, and is it so very different from traditional methods?

Above: Horse and rider in harmony: Charles Wilson riding Coloured Cob Drummer Boy (Ben).

Natural horsemanship and 'horse whispering'

In the last chapter I referred to the idea that horses should do things for us because we want them to. This is based on the concept of making the horse see us as the 'herd leader' or 'dominant horse'; the assumption is that if we can achieve this it will do as we wish, because the herd leader supposedly controls the movement of the other horses in a herd, just as an individual horse exercising dominance over another horse will get the other to move away. However, trainers who advocate this seldom explain exactly what they mean when they describe a horse as 'dominant'. Do they mean that a particular horse prevails over the others? Well, if so, in

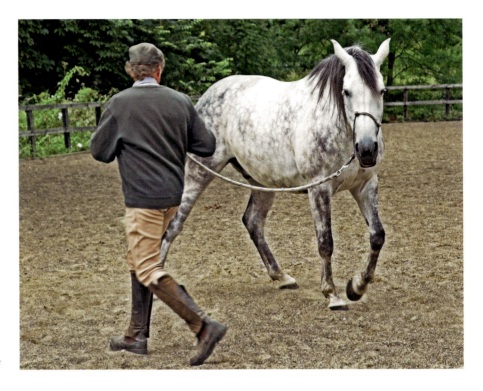

Right: Natural horsemanship: working from the ground.

Below: Classical in-hand work is an excellent way of relaxing and suppling the horse, building a rapport with him and preparing him for ridden work.

what contexts? It is very rare indeed to find one horse that *always* prevails in *all* circumstances. Or do they simply mean aggressive? If so, then they have failed to observe that horses avoid aggressive bullies wherever they can, that aggression only works in a very limited way, and that in horses it is normally a response to a specific situation – usually negative.

Many trainers who use the term 'dominant' say their methods do not involve aggression towards the horse. Yet the same trainers often describe in great detail the 'pecking orders' ruled by a so-called 'alpha horse', which are supposed to be an organizing feature of equine society, and on which they supposedly base their methods. But a 'pecking order' is nothing more or less than a hierarchy of aggression! And, as we saw in Chapter 3, when we look at the systematic studies that have been carried out into the lives of feral horses, we see that such a social organization is virtually non-existent when horses are left to their own devices and allowed to form natural family groups.

It is important that we understand this, because much received wisdom in the horse world – and not only that concerned with 'natural horsemanship' – is based on the idea that horses must have a 'pecking order' (as if they were chickens) and that we must train and manage them accordingly – with ourselves, of course, at the top of the 'pecking order'. This idea seems to work for some people, which is why it persists and why so many people make it the basis for their training. However, with many horses – especially the more sensitive and reactive types – it can lead to real problems.

Creating conflict

If we do as so many trainers insist we should, and try to make ourselves the equivalent of the so-called 'alpha horse' we actually create conflict in the mind of the horse. If we observe carefully what happens when one horse threatens another, we can see that the horse being threatened does not roll over and submit the way a dog might. The horse will either go away – which is not very helpful, as we want it to stay with us while we attempt to train it – or, depending on the individual, respond with aggression.

So if we try to imitate a dominant horse by using aggressive body language, the horse we are interacting with may want to leave (but be prevented from doing so because it is being restrained in some way) or it may become aggressive towards us. As we saw in Chapter 3, the only time dominance really becomes an issue in natural horse society is when horses are competing over some resource. And, as we also saw, this is not a situation that arises very frequently. The point is we are not competing with our horses, so why should they accept our dominance? Given that there is no one horse that directs the movements of the group, why should they accept our leadership, or give us their respect?

The horse that learns to keep its distance from the trainer because, for example, a rope is twirled or shaken in its face, is not necessarily doing so because it has learned to 'respect' the trainer (however the latter defines 'respect') or come to accept the person as the herd 'leader'. No, it will do so because it has learned that the rope twirling or shaking, which most horses want to avoid, will stop once it has done so. This is nothing other than negative reinforcement, no matter what else people may choose to call it. So regardless of what trainers say is happening, or what they think is happening, they are using the same principles that have been in use for as long as people have been training animals.

The horse that learns to keep its distance from the trainer because, for example, a rope is twirled or shaken in its face, is not necessarily doing so because it has learned to 'respect' the trainer.

The best of both worlds

This is not to say that there are not some very fine trainers working with methods they term 'natural horsemanship'. These trainers, regardless of how they describe what they do, often bring together the best of the new methods with the best of more traditional methods. Such trainers emphasize – as indeed do the best of the more traditional trainers – the need to gain the horse's mental co-operation. They do this by initially working from the ground, using body language that tells the horse they are calm, relaxed and confident. Some trainers describe this as 'damping down' their own energy levels. This might involve breathing out and relaxing their stance, which encourages the horse to stand still. Conversely, by bringing their own energy up – which might be nothing more than adopting a more erect posture, taking a deep breath and assuming a more alert and positive demeanour – the trainer can raise the horse's level of activity. By raising and lowering their own energy levels in this way, the trainer can move the horse around and ask it to stop without doing a great deal other than gently asking, by a feel on the lead rope or a slight movement of the hand. In this way the trainer begins to establish a 'connection' with the horse.

Below: Trainer Charles Wilson is riding without reins and using subtle shifts of weight and body position to ask the horse to change direction, bend, etc.

This is of course a greatly over-simplified description. The concept of controlling the horse in this way is based on *feel*, just like the best kind of ridden work. This type of work from the ground is very similar to the kind of in-hand work traditionally carried out in the various schools of classical horsemanship. Comparatively few people, other than devotees of classical riding, are familiar with these techniques. As the term suggests, in-hand work is carried out from the ground, with the trainer in close contact with the horse but the technique varies according to the school of training being followed. For example, at the Spanish Riding School the horse wears a cavesson, whereas in Portugal it wears a simple snaffle bridle.

In-hand work

In essence, the Portuguese method is very simple, although more difficult than it looks at

Above: Riding without reins.

first sight. The trainer stands at the horse's shoulder, holding the outside rein over the horse's neck, and the other hand holds the inside rein, close to the bit. The trainer walks alongside the horse and directs the latter in what can best be described as a kind of stately dance. The horse may be asked to walk forward, step back, halt, perform a shoulder-in either in a straight line or in a circle around the handler, as well as any combination of these.

In-hand work carried out like this can be invaluable in helping to relax and supple the horse in preparation for ridden work and to loosen up horses when their joints have stiffened up. For the horse the benefits are psychological as well as physical as the intimacy of the work helps to create a close bond between horse and trainer, and the trainer, working at close quarters, can gauge the horse's reactions more readily than from a distance.

There are other similarities between 'natural horsemanship' and classical riding. Many devotees of the former advocate using the rider's weight and leg aids, rather than steering the horse with the reins, to direct the horse where they want it to go. Yet this is just what classical riders have been doing since the days of Xenophon!

All this shows that there is not really all that much difference between the best kind of traditional horsemanship and the best of 'natural horsemanship'. The most logical approach to different training methods is surely not to follow any one method slavishly, but to take from the various approaches whatever works well, while motivating the horse not only to give of its best, but to *want* to do so.

Understanding the principles

Whatever approach we adopt, we need to look beyond the various 'labels' that people like to put on different training methods, and understand the principles we are putting into practice. If we do not, we may end up punishing the horse even when we do not intend to, or using too much negative reinforcement.

If we pile on the pressure too much, and forget to release it when the horse has complied, then our use of negative reinforcement has become oppressive and amounts to coercion.

For example, we might adopt methods that rely on the use of pressure. However, if we pile on the pressure too much, and forget to release it when the horse has complied, then our use of negative reinforcement has become oppressive and amounts to coercion, which may produce a compliant horse but may also cause it to break down psychologically.

Or we might be using positive reinforcement in an inappropriate way, for example by conditioning horses to act in ways that are actually harmful to them. For instance, we might think it is very clever to teach our horse to perform advanced dressage movements by using clicker training, but not realise that by teaching it to perform such movements without the necessary suppling and strengthening exercises which form the whole basis of dressage, we are actually damaging it physically.

Many of the new breed of trainers advocate 'making the wrong thing difficult' for the horse. This may help the horse to understand what we *don't* want it to do, but it does nothing to help it to understand what we *do* want it to do. It is surely better to think in terms of 'making the right thing easy'.

Dealing with problems

When we come across problems in training, it is tempting to see these as evidence that the horse is 'trying it on' with us. We are often told that we must not let the horse 'get away' with something, or it will start to think it has the upper hand. Some trainers even go so far as to say that when this happens, the horse 'scores points' in its mind. In fact, it is

Above: The highly collected advanced movements, such as the piaffe shown here, are very demanding.

extremely unlikely that anything of the kind is happening. As Chapter 3 showed, the only horses that have to think in these terms are stallions either defending their mares or seeking to take over a band. But in a training situation even a stallion is not in competition with humans for some resource – so why should it think it needs to gain the 'upper hand' with us?

The only reason horses would want to get their own way is because, not being driven by the human work ethic, they want an easy life. If they can find ways of doing things in a manner that minimizes effort on their part, they will do so. There is nothing sinister in this; it simply means that instead of wasting time worrying that our horses are plotting against us or trying to gain the upper hand, we should instead be trying to find ways of making training – and anything else we may ask of them – rewarding enough that they will comply willingly and even with enthusiasm.

Chapter *6*

How horses cope with the demands of competition

In the wild horses would normally only gallop in order to flee from real or perceived danger.

RIDERS SOMETIMES describe their successful competition horses as having a 'will to win'. But as we saw in Chapter 3, horses are among the least competitive of animals – so does winning *really* mean anything to them in the context of equestrian competitions, or is this just a projection of human ambitions on to them?

Do horses understand competition?

There is no doubt that certain horses appear to understand that they have done well in competition and this is most probably because they pick up signals from their riders and the people around them. Horses are perfectly capable of learning to recognize signs of pleasure in the humans around them. So signs of approval may spur them on, figuratively speaking, to make the same or even greater efforts the next time out.

It is extremely unlikely, though, that their efforts result from any competitive spirit for although some horses seem to like to be at the front when running about with others in the field, there may be many reasons for this that have nothing to do with any sense of competition. They may simply be responding to the excitement of the moment, or it could also be that being at the front gives them a sense of security. In the wild horses would normally only gallop in order to flee from real or perceived danger, and the horse that put the greatest distance between itself and danger would be most likely to survive!

Can horses enjoy competitive disciplines?

So can horses actually enjoy equestrian competitions, even if they have no intrinsic meaning for them?

If they are properly prepared, do not suffer from stress while loading and travelling (covered in Chapter 7) and are not subjected to abusive training methods or asked to perform beyond their capabilities, then I believe horses can certainly enjoy competitions. For young horses, going to shows can be a great, fun experience. Not only do they get to see different places, they may also become acquainted with other horses as well as humans other than their riders and handlers. They become habituated to a huge variety of different sights and sounds, including other species of animal not normally encountered in their everyday lives. Horses accustomed in this way to a wide range of stimuli are less likely to become spooky and unmanageable when ridden out in unfamiliar places. Moreover, they are not so likely to become over-excited when meeting other horses.

However, much depends on how the individual horse has been brought up and managed. Those that are socially naïve, perhaps because they have not been given sufficient opportunity to socialize with other horses

Above: Shows can be a great way of introducing young horses to a variety of new sights and sounds. This heavy horse foal waits patiently in line without fuss.

in groups of mixed ages and sexes, or that have been bullied by other horses (usually for the reasons described in Chapter 3), may be intimidated when encountering other horses at shows. They may react with aggression or by 'freezing', or in some cases refusing to move at all until other horses have moved away. This can be dangerous as well as upsetting for their riders as well as other horses. As always, prevention is better than cure; before going to competitions, horses should be introduced to as many other horses as possible within a controlled environment, so that shows will not become too stressful.

Competitions represent a deviation from a daily routine, so it is scarcely surprising that horses that are used to such a routine frequently become agitated and excited.

In Chapter 3, I pointed out that horses left to their own devices do not have routines as such; they are, however, creatures of habit. Hence, in a domestic setting horses that have become accustomed to routines created for them by their human caretakers are often upset when these are disrupted, not because they actually need such a routine, but because once established it has become a habit. Competitions represent a deviation from a daily routine, so it is scarcely surprising that horses that are used to such a routine frequently become agitated and excited. Seasoned competitors such as top-class showjumpers or eventers may spend a good part of the year travelling to and from competitions, but because they have become accustomed to this way of life, they are less likely to suffer from stress-related illnesses as a result of changes in routine. Nevertheless, such illnesses are still quite common even among horses that are used to the stresses of competition so wise competitors keep a close eye on their horses for signs of tension and stress.

Some equestrian competitive disciplines demand the horse has a high level of physical fitness and this is particularly the case with eventing and endurance. Others, such as dressage and showing, require presence and sparkle as well as discipline and poise. All of these requirements make demands upon horses that may result in physical and/or behavioural problems.

Conflicting demands

In addition to physical stresses, many equestrian activities ask horses to behave in ways that may run counter to their sense of security. For example, as we saw in Chapter 3 horses normally maintain a distance around themselves (the personal space) into which only close friends and family are allowed. The intrusion of a strange horse into this personal space can create a great deal of stress. Yet in some equestrian sports such as racing and polo this intrusion cannot be avoided. For

example, the racehorse cannot help but invade the personal space of other runners, especially if the field is large. In a game of polo the horse must not mind being in close proximity to other horses, and he must learn to put up with being 'ridden off', which often involves actual physical contact as one horse shoulders another out of his way. Not all horses can accept that, however, and many that otherwise have the ideal physical build and athletic ability for polo, nevertheless fail to make the grade because they cannot tolerate being pushed around by other horses in this manner. One of my own horses, an Arabian gelding, would have made an ideal polo pony but for this one factor: even in a practice arena, if another horse approaches too closely my gelding will quickly dodge out of the way.

There is now a huge variety of equestrian sports, and for this reason we cannot consider all of them; instead we will take a brief look at some of those which have gained worldwide popularity, namely dressage,

Above: Polo ponies must not object to being 'ridden off' or shouldered out of the way.

showjumping, eventing and endurance riding, with a nod in the direction of showing. The comments relating to these disciplines are broadly applicable to many other equestrian sports.

Whatever the discipline, the ridden horse that is to take part in competition needs to be prepared both physically and mentally; the foundation for this is *dressage*.

Dressage

Throughout the horse world, dressage is generally regarded as a competitive discipline in which the horse is required to perform specific movements in a prescribed form, but comparatively few people think of it as having any other purpose. Yet originally dressage meant nothing more than training ('dressing', from the French *dresser*) for ridden work. A trained horse was referred to as being 'dressed' and although in the 17th and 18th centuries the masters of equitation and their pupils liked to display their horses' prowess and their own riding ability in the

Below: Competitive dressage is a very demanding discipline.

advanced movements (*piaffe, passage* and so on) of the High School, these displays had not yet been turned into competitions. That came much later, as army officers of the late 19th and early 20th centuries devised ways of rewarding excellence in the training of their horses.

We might think that all this is pointless and that it would be better just to let horses carry themselves in whatever way they find comfortable. However, this would not necessarily be best for the horse. If we want to ride our horses – which is the case with most of us who have them – then it is not kind or ethical to let them simply slop around any old how, without making some effort to train them to carry themselves in such a way that the rider becomes less of a burden. The great German master Gustav Steinbrecht wrote in *The Gymnasium of the Horse* (originally published as *Gymnasium des Pferdes* in 1885 and translated from the original by Helen K. Gibble, Xenophon Press 1995) that the aims of dressage are 'to develop the natural forces and capabilities of the horse to perfection through gradual and appropriate exercises'. This is the real purpose of dressage, and from this point of view it is – or should be – the foundation for all other disciplines, although most people would think of it as *flatwork* rather than dressage.

However, now that dressage has become a discipline in its own right, greater precision is demanded of horse and rider, and tests have to be

Above: Training tests devised by Classical Riding Club founder Sylvia Loch are more 'horse friendly' than standard dressage tests (see the list of useful organizations and websites on pages 140–141).

ridden accurately to markers, in a correct form. This means that training for competitive dressage makes great demands on the horse, which – as we saw in Chapter 2 – is much more inclined to an easy life. Training involves many strenuous exercises designed to supple and strengthen the muscles the horse will have to use in order to perform the various movements. If the training is correct, these exercises are exactly the same as those that should form the foundation for any ridden work, except that at higher levels of dressage competition the training becomes the equivalent of a kind of higher education for the horse.

The dressage horse is expected to be obedient under saddle and there is nothing wrong with this in itself, as an unruly horse is an unsafe horse.

Unfortunately, in their understandable wish to progress quickly, too many riders make the mistake of asking their horse to perform advanced movements before it is either physically or mentally ready. This can lead to resistance, which can take many forms. The most obvious ones are swishing the tail, grinding the teeth (both of which may be penalized in dressage tests) and getting the tongue over the bit in an attempt to obtain relief. However, there are many other forms of resistance that all too often are mistaken for stubbornness or unwillingness on the part of the horse. These may include stiffness throughout the body – but most commonly in the neck and at the poll – reluctance to move forward, bearing down on the bit, getting behind the bit (often mistaken for a good 'outline'), rearing, attempting to run away, and various other behaviours usually labelled 'misbehaviour'. For a discussion of 'outline' see my book *Realize Your Horse's True Potential* (J.A. Allen 2003).

This is not the only source of potential problems for the dressage horse. On the one hand, horses do not need to be 'taught' the dressage movements as they already know how to perform them all, from flying changes to the extreme collected movements such as the *piaffe*. Even the least naturally talented horse is incomparably more athletic than most of us realise, although of course some horses have more natural ability than others. On the other hand, when horses are asked to perform all these movements calmly, with precision and in a controlled manner, they have to suppress many of their normal instincts. The dressage horse is expected to be obedient under saddle and there is nothing wrong with this in itself, as an unruly horse is an unsafe horse. But dressage horses often have their natural behaviour suppressed to the extent that they become almost robotic – or the opposite may be true. Part of the presence and sparkle seen in the most impressive-looking dressage horses is the result of a natural exuberance which is encouraged by the best riders, albeit not allowed to spill over into unruliness. However, some dressage horses are so wound up that they seem about to explode.

The resulting tension can mar an otherwise impressive test, but unfortunately all too often judges overlook this where the horse has naturally impressive paces.

This is a problem often experienced with event horses in the dressage phase. These horses are supremely fit and ready to run. Thus they often find it difficult to remain calm even in the relatively subdued atmosphere of the dressage arena – which is why some of the top names in eventing history have had some exciting experiences when participating in dressage tests!

Showing classes

This kind of explosiveness is often seen in horses taking part in certain in-hand breed classes and Arabians and Welsh Cobs in particular are noted for their fiery in-hand displays. However, the methods sometimes used to evoke this kind of display are often unacceptable. Show horses are frequently over-fed with feedstuffs high in energy or they may be kept confined to a stable for prolonged periods before a show. Sometimes

Below: Some in-hand classes, especially those for Welsh Cobs, are noted for their fiery displays.

Right: Not all in-hand classes feature extreme behaviour; many are noted for the good manners of their exhibits.

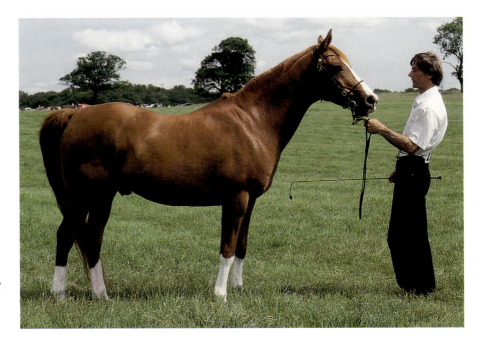

Below: Horses in ridden showing classes must show good manners as well as sparkle and presence.

they are even shut up in the dark. Some may be trained by methods that involve abuse of the whip, or other instruments of coercion such as fire-extinguishers or even cattle prods. It is a telling comment on training methods all too often used on show horses that a number of breed societies have found it necessary to formulate show rules forbidding, for example, the use of whips capable of delivering an electric shock to the horse!

It is not at all uncommon in certain in-hand classes to see horses that are quite obviously terrified of the whip. Their fear is evident in their body language (as described in Chapter 1) and their response – avoidance – to the handler's presence. Even where there is no actual whip abuse in the showring, there are frequent examples of what I call 'passive whip abuse' – where the handler constantly waves a whip at the horse, presumably to remind it of what it may expect if it does not do as the handler wishes.

Since this kind of whip-waving is frequently accompanied by jerking on the lead-rein, or by a constant pushing and pulling of the horse – even when it is standing perfectly still and, to all appearances, behaving itself – the horse cannot possibly be expected to know what is required of it. Some will put up with such bullying and confusion, but there are many others that will not, and the resulting behavioural problems, which may range from withdrawal into a shut-down state of mechanical obedience to sudden outbursts of explosive violence, can render a horse virtually unmanageable.

In some breed classes the handlers actively encourage their horses to misbehave in the showring, whether in the mistaken belief that this makes them look more impressive, or as a tactic to distract rivals' horses. Some horses, especially stallions, become so overwrought that their behaviour becomes dangerous, especially when they are actually encouraged to rear in the showring. Horses incited to behave in this way have been known to get loose and cause injury to themselves and to other horses, not to mention to handlers and spectators.

Of course there are many showing classes in which extremes of behaviour are not encouraged and are actually frowned upon. The in-hand classes at many breed shows can be models of good behaviour and the horses taking part in such classes generally appear comparatively stress-free. In most ridden showing classes horses are required to display good manners as well as sparkle and presence, but although their way of going must show good form the demands on them are nothing like as

Some horses, especially stallions, become so overwrought that their behaviour becomes dangerous, especially when they are actually encouraged to rear in the showring.

intense as those made on dressage horses. Many that are nervous in the isolation of the dressage arena are calm and level-headed in showing classes, where they are in the comforting company of other horses. Provided, as always, that they are trained and ridden correctly and with consideration, horses generally appear to enjoy participating in ridden showing classes.

Showjumping

This is one discipline for which many horses have a natural physical aptitude. However, it is one that they may find very daunting and, quite frankly, from their point of view, really rather pointless. Feral or free-ranging horses when faced with an obstacle they could easily jump over will generally go round it if they can; after all, why waste energy? Yet the ease with which horses can be taught to go over jumps has made the discipline of showjumping one of the most enduringly popular of equestrian sports.

Below: When a horse takes off over a jump, he has to remember the details of the jump in order to clear it with his hind feet.

In their own enthusiasm for jumping, riders may fail to realize that their horse does not necessarily share the same enthusiasm. All horses that are sound and in good health are physically capable of jumping and some are naturally more athletic in this respect than others. Yet even where a horse has a natural aptitude for jumping it may find it a frightening experience. It must not only learn to approach the jump in such a way that it can judge the height and spread, it must also remember those details accurately so that it knows how to clear the jump with its hind feet. Some horses may end up catching their hind legs painfully a number of times before they learn how to do this – an experience which can put them off jumping altogether if it happens too often. In addition, many green horses do not know how to land properly.

Even when a horse lands correctly, one of its forelegs will, at the moment of landing, have to take the entire weight of horse and rider. For a medium-sized horse this could be anything from 400 to 550 kg (884–1,216 lbs), which is a great deal for one foot to support! It is very

Below: As a horse lands after a jump, the leading forefoot has to sustain the horse's entire weight.

Above: Showjumping can be a very demanding discipline.

easy for a horse landing badly to jar its front legs, neck and spine – and this jarring may not only result in injuries but also make the horse reluctant to tackle jumps at all.

This is why horses must be introduced gradually to the idea of jumping, and must never be over-faced. The latter is true at any time, but this is especially the case with green horses. If they are made to tackle fences that are too big, too soon, they will quickly become anxious about the whole process, and may start to rush their fences in an effort to get it over with as quickly as possible. This is often mistaken for enthusiasm, and all kinds of stratagems are devised to train such horses not to rush jumps. The commonest of these consists of circling before a jump, the idea being that a horse cannot rush if it is coming out of a circle. However, this does nothing to alleviate its anxiety – it simply makes it difficult for it to deal with its problem. The horse that is badly afflicted in this way may then progress to running out at fences, napping (in some cases refusing to enter the ring altogether), rearing or – in some extreme cases – running away.

The answer is not to persist in trying to deal with the problem by simply masking it, but to go right back to the beginning, starting if necessary with going over trotting poles, at a walk to begin with and then at a trot.

If the horse rushes even then, the rider should revert to working at the walk. Once it is happily going over these, the horse can be asked to progress to raised trotting poles, gradually moving on to cavalletti (if the rider is experienced with these and comfortable about using them) and then to small cross-poles.

All of this is not to say that horses cannot enjoy jumping. On the contrary, some appear to be genuinely enthusiastic about it, approaching jumps confidently, without rushing, and without having to be encouraged by the rider. Some will jump voluntarily; I have known a number of horses that, having jumped out of a field, whether in order to join companions from which they have been separated or in order to attain some other objective, will then continue to jump out and then back in again, for no apparent reason other than the fact that they can. Such horses seem to become exhilarated by the act of jumping – rather like many humans. However, such horses are comparatively rare; most, even when confined to a field or paddock with a low fence that they could easily jump, will not attempt to do so. This is perhaps just as well.

Eventing

Eventing, or more properly Horse Trials, evolved from the military competitions which used to be held in 19th and early 20th century Europe, as a means of testing the correctness of training of officers' mounts and the abilities of their riders. Because it included dressage, jumping and cross-country disciplines, it was an all-round test of the abilities of both horse and rider. Modern horse trials may consist of One Day Events, where all three tests are held on the same day; Two Day Events, with dressage and showjumping taking place on the same day and the cross-country component on the next; and Three Day Events, widely regarded as the supreme test of horse and rider. In a Three Day Event the dressage is held on the first day; the cross-country round takes place on the second day, and the showjumping on the third. The second day used to include Roads and Tracks sections as well as a steeplechase, but these elements have been gradually phased out.

All the elements of horse trials are regarded as important, but attention tends to focus on the cross-country element, perhaps because this is the most exciting and demanding part of the competition.

Many horses and ponies seem to enjoy cross-country jumping much more than they do showjumping. This may be because the obstacles are

All the elements of horse trials are regarded as important, but attention tends to focus on the cross-country element, perhaps because this is the most exciting and demanding part of the competition.

more natural looking (except at the higher levels of competition, where all kinds of bizarre obstacles may be encountered) and the horse is not expected to make as many twists and turns in quick succession as in a showjumping round. The surroundings are also more inviting. Galloping over open ground, or cantering and trotting through woodland are much more congenial to most horses than jumping over coloured poles in a relatively confined space. Hence, provided they are not rushed or over-faced, even horses that have previously been reluctant to jump may prove surprisingly willing to do so over a well-constructed cross-country course.

Having said this, some horses that would unhesitatingly follow others over even quite

formidable obstacles in the hunting field may balk at jumping the same obstacles solo. Such horses need tactful and sympathetic yet positive riding and handling to give them confidence.

Above: Event horses have to be very fit.

Endurance riding

Of all the equestrian competitive disciplines, endurance or long-distance riding is perhaps the one which horses find the most congenial. Although they have to be fit and the sport demands a great deal of them by way of exertion, horses are not required to perform the kind of intricate manoeuvres found in dressage tests, nor do they generally have to jump obstacles that they would avoid if left to their own devices. Most horses enjoy hacking out, especially in company, and for a properly prepared horse a long-distance ride may simply seem like an extension of a lengthy hack, albeit rather faster and over more demanding terrain than usual.

Opposite above: The cross-country phase is the most popular aspect of a three-day event.

Even the preparation for a long-distance ride may be more enjoyable for the horse than the equivalent preparation for disciplines such as dressage

Opposite below: The obstacles on a cross-country course are usually more natural than those in a showjumping round.

Right: Many horses appear to enjoy endurance or long-distance riding.

or showjumping. In some parts of the world the training takes place over similar terrain to the eventual ride, while in others it may consist of riding out on roads or through fields. Many endurance horses may not even regard this as work!

Some horses do fret and refuse to eat before a long-distance ride, which could indicate that they may be finding the demands of the sport too much for them. On the other hand, many others seem to find the challenge of long-distance events stimulating and even relaxing. Ann Hyland, who has competed successfully in endurance events both nationally and internationally, and is the founder of the Endurance Horse and Pony Society of Great Britain, remarks in *The Endurance Horse* (J.A. Allen 1988) as follows:

'Horses suffering from flightiness, tension, lack of concentration, playful shying or just plain boredom are often completely changed by a challenging season. During this time they come to realize they have a job to do and need to concentrate all their energies into producing maximum effort with minimum fatigue. Work is also an anodyne for some really nervous horses who unwind as the miles roll out.'

So although competition may be stressful for horses and may involve activities that require them to act in ways that run contrary to what they would do naturally, they can adapt well to it, and even find it enjoyable – provided their trainers and riders do not make unreasonable demands of them or ignore their fears and uncertainties.

As long as riders and trainers remember that the horse is a being in its own right (albeit one with four legs and a tail) and as such deserves the same kind of respect and consideration one would show a valued human colleague, the partnerships forged in competition can be rewarding and satisfying for both parties. As a very great horseman, Nuno Oliveira, observed in *Reflections on Equestrian Art* (J.A. Allen), 'Make him a companion, and not a slave, then you will see what a true friend he is.'

Below: Riding out in the fields is a good way to get horses fit while keeping them relaxed.

Chapter 7

The travel stress factor

Below: Trailers of this type are very common but may be cramped and too unstable, especially for larger horses.

THROUGHOUT THE history of horses' association with humans, they have always been required to travel long distances. Of course, before the advent of railways and, later on, that of motorized horse transport, they would have had to travel naturally – on foot. And, provided they were fit, fed well enough to provide them with sufficient energy and not ridden to the point of exhaustion, such journeys were seldom a problem, because as we have seen they are adapted to almost continual movement in their natural state. Thus it was

usually due only to human carelessness or neglect that horses ended up injured or dying on such long journeys.

Above: Modern horseboxes can be very luxurious, but horses may still find them daunting.

Stress induced by loading and travelling

Nowadays things are very different and the pace of life is such that horses often need to be transported quickly and efficiently, whether for racing, competition, training, going to stud or simply travelling to a new home. So we might think that our modern forms of horse transport are much easier and less tiring for the horse. Wrong!

Travelling in an enclosed railway car, a horsebox or by air can be extremely stressful, for a number of reasons. Injuries sustained while loading and travelling are distressingly common and these are frequently the root cause of behavioural problems. However, very often these problems arise even in the absence of any actual injury. Virtually every demonstration given by trainers specializing in behaviour modification includes at least one horse that is reluctant to go into a horsebox or trailer – or refuses outright, while at shows and competitions one may see any number of competitors beside themselves with frustration trying to get a horse up the ramp into its trailer or horsebox.

Above: Horses on an open trailer: this mode of transport may be unconventional and possibly hazardous, but some horses could find it more congenial than travelling in a closed lorry or trailer.

Understanding equine behaviour and physiology helps us to see why loading and travelling can create problems. As we saw in Chapters 1 and 2, horses need the freedom to move around and to escape from situations they may perceive to be potentially dangerous. If they are prevented from doing so they may feel trapped and powerless, which can have a very detrimental effect on their physical and mental wellbeing. If being stabled for prolonged periods of time can affect them adversely, how much more must they be affected by being confined in a horsebox or trailer (float), with its narrow spaces and dim interior?

To make things worse, the thing moves, compelling the horse to shift its weight as it tries to balance. It is an instructive experience to watch – from the safety of the living compartment, if there is one – a horse travelling in a conventional horsebox. One can see then just how much of an effort some horses have to make to steady themselves against the movement of the vehicle, and how upset many of them become as a result of this and of being trapped in a small space. By the way, for safety reasons, standing in the horse compartment of a trailer is not recommended, and in some countries is actually illegal.

So if we put ourselves in the horse's place we can see why so many of them are reluctant to go into a horsebox or trailer in the first place. Not only do many of them find the experience of being transported worrying, they are often frightened by the unsteadiness of the ramp they have to use in order to enter the thing in the first place. No horse likes to feel unsteady on its feet; a flight animal such as the horse needs to feel in control of its own feet at all times, so that it can get away quickly if danger threatens. Going into a horsebox or trailer, and travelling in one, must therefore make the horse feel as if this control has been taken away from it. So it is small wonder therefore that so many horses sweat up while being transported.

The effects of orientation during travel

A considerable amount of research has been carried out into the effects of orientation within a trailer or horsebox. Approximately 60 per cent of a horse's weight is carried by his forehand at rest but when the animal faces *into* the direction of travel, the vehicle's movement forces it to brace itself using its hindquarters in order to avoid being thrown forward. Although it is desirable for ridden horses to take more weight on their hindquarters in order to relieve the forehand, it is asking too much of them to maintain this in a stationary position for any length of time. After a while the horse may try to relieve its tired and aching muscles by shifting about, which decreases the stability of the vehicle. This in turn can upset the horse, which may then shift around even more, further decreasing stability. In some cases horses can become so distressed by this increasing instability that they panic and injure themselves, but even if this does not happen, they may arrive at their destination tired and stressed.

Dealing with problems

Considering all the factors outlined above, it might seem obvious why problems arise with loading and transporting horses. Yet many people persist in thinking of such problems as some kind of disobliging awkwardness on the part of the horse; all too often they will say the horse is just being awkward or naughty or 'trying it on', or 'he's lacking in respect for the handler'. Instead of trying to understand the horse's fears and devise ways of overcoming them, they will attempt to coerce the horse into loading and then, when that fails, seek the help of various 'experts' to get their reluctant loader sorted out. Unfortunately, few of these 'experts' seem to consider the *cause* of the horse's fears either.

No horse likes to feel unsteady on its feet; a flight animal such as the horse needs to feel in control of its own feet at all times, so that it can get away quickly if danger threatens.

Instead, they tend to focus simply on the result, which is to get the horse into the horsebox or trailer. They disregard the fact that while they may have achieved their aim, they have not tackled the cause of the problem, which may then resurface at a later date.

Methods of persuasion

There are many methods of persuading reluctant loaders to go into a horsebox or trailer, but too many of them involve the use of a greater or lesser degree of force or coercion. When brute force is used it may take the form of trying to haul the horse up the ramp – a rather pointless exercise, given the sheer strength of horses, although sometimes a number of burly men can achieve a degree of success. Sometimes the handler may exert a pull on the headcollar, and if the horse takes a step forward the handler slackens the tension on the rope. This is supposed to constitute a 'reward' for taking a step forward, but as we saw in Chapter 4, this is really an example of negative reinforcement. It may persuade the horse that moving forward is better than enduring the pressure of the headcollar, but it does nothing to make going up the ramp into the trailer or horsebox an inviting prospect.

The same applies to the commonly used method of putting a lunge-line around the horse's hindquarters and exerting pressure to make it move forwards up the ramp. This may work with some reluctant loaders whose dislike of the ramp is not strong enough to make it battle against the lunge-line, but with some horses this procedure could provoke a panic. Such horses might rear up and/or leap about in an attempt to escape the pressure of the lunge line, or they might rush forward up the ramp with such violence that they injure themselves. Either way, the risk of injury to horse and handlers is considerable. This is also the case with another popular method – the application of a broom to the horse's hindquarters in an attempt to make it move forward. Most horses will indeed move away from the unpleasant sensation (as I expect you or I would, too), but whether they will move in the desired direction is open to question. Some will lash out violently with their hind feet, and all too many handlers using this method have been kicked or otherwise injured.

Certain adherents of various schools of 'natural horsemanship' practise some methods that supposedly avoid the use of coercion. These methods usually involve gaining control of the horse's feet, by moving the animal around and away from the handler. Sometimes the horse is made to go in

Above: This horse is hesitant about entering the horsebox. The slope of the ramp has been adjusted to encourage him; soon after this was taken he stepped into the box.

small circles around the handler, who may make hissing noises and wave their hands or twirl a rope in the horse's face. The horse keeps moving in order to avoid the handler and/or the twirling rope and is gradually moved closer and closer to the trailer or horsebox until it has no option but to step on the ramp even if it must then step off again. Eventually the handler manoeuvres the horse so that it can go straight up the ramp and into the trailer.

However, none of these procedures does anything to overcome the horse's fears. On the contrary, the use of such forceful methods may actually increase those fears, by confirming the horse's suspicions that horseboxes and trailers are places where unpleasant things happen.

Some horses eventually 'give in' and go into the horsebox or trailer simply to gain relief from whatever method is being used to persuade them to comply.

Some horses eventually 'give in' and go into the horsebox or trailer simply to gain relief from whatever method is being used to persuade them to comply. Others – perhaps stronger characters, or those for which the fear or dislike of the horsebox is greater than their fear or dislike of the trainer's method – may resist far more. This resistance can be so stubborn that the horse becomes dangerous; this may be especially the case with high-spirited stallions. Attempts to coerce such individuals may end in injury to horse or handler, or both – and this is unacceptable and unnecessary. There are ways of getting such horses to co-operate that do not involve coercion of any kind. These methods may take more time (although this is not necessarily the case) but they are more truly effective as well as being more pleasant for all concerned.

Persuasion without coercion

These methods make use of techniques based on making the experience as rewarding for the horse as possible rather than gaining physical control of it, while minimizing any negative aspects of loading and travelling.

Perhaps the easiest way to introduce a horse to a horsebox or trailer is to let it investigate it for itself. Most horses are curious about anything unusual, even though they may initially be very wary, so make use of this natural inquisitiveness. Ideally, the ramp should have a non-slip matting surface and be almost level, so the horse does not have to negotiate too much of a slope. It should also be as solid as possible – so the horse does not feel insecure when it steps onto it. If the ground is uneven, use wedges under the ramp to stop it flexing when it starts to bear the horse's weight. As regards the box or trailer, the interior should be as light as possible (if there are interior lights, these should

Left: This horse looks relaxed in his travelling compartment.

be switched on) and any interior partitions opened as fully as possible to create more space. Placing a pile of hay or a bucket of feed at the back will tempt the horse to investigate; I have found that this works very well with horses that have not previously had a bad experience with horseboxes.

Once the horse is happy to go in and out of the box on its own, an attempt can be made to lead it in and out. When it accepts this without resistance and remains calm when the doors are closed on it, the next test is to see if it maintains this calm when the engine is started and/or when the trailer starts to move. To begin with the box or trailer should be moved only a few metres, and sharp turns should be avoided. Once the horse is happy to travel short distances, with the distance being gradually increased, it can be taken on a longer journey, which should still be kept relatively short – say, two or three kilometres. Having a steady travelling companion accompany the horse may help to give it confidence.

Taking it slowly

I must emphasize that initial success at any stage is just the beginning. Each step in the whole process must be taken slowly and the next stage not attempted until the current one has been consolidated. This may seem like a long, drawn-out way of doing things, but patience and extra time taken now can help the horse to build confidence about travelling and prevent problems later on. Exactly the same applies when rebuilding a horse's confidence after a bad experience in a horsebox or trailer.

Travelling facing the rear

The research referred to earlier in this chapter has shown that when horses travel facing backwards – with their hindquarters facing the direction of travel – they are able to stabilize themselves more easily and so are less likely to find the experience of travelling stressful. Most modern horseboxes have partitions arranged in a 'herringbone' pattern, enabling horses to travel at an angle facing slightly to the rear of the horsebox and the majority appear to find this much more congenial than the old forward-facing compartments. Rear-facing travel in trailers has been much slower to evolve, but there are now a number of companies manufacturing such trailers (it must be emphasized that forward-facing trailers cannot simply be adapted for rear-facing travel as this affects the balance of the trailer). There are now many excellent, spacious trailers

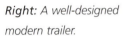

Right: A well-designed modern trailer.

and horseboxes with side-loading ramps which allow horses to travel facing the rear. There are even trailers available with low, secure loading platforms which enable the horse to step onto the platform and then be turned round and backed into the trailer. This is much easier than trying to back a horse up a ramp and is actually quite easy to teach horses. It is, after all, the way horses have been backed between the shafts of certain types of carriage for centuries! For more information on platform-loading trailers, visit http://www.animaltransportation.com/.

If in spite of all preparation problems do arise, however, it is vital to remember the following:
• Most problems concerning loading and travelling arise from fear or discomfort.
• Any attempt to deal with such problems without addressing the cause will merely mask the problem. It will not cure it.
• The horse that has developed a fear or dislike of loading and/or travelling cannot be expected to overcome its concerns overnight. Sometimes lengthy rehabilitation may be necessary.

Whatever the situation, patience – as in every aspect of dealing with horses – is not only a virtue, it is essential. Nothing of value can be achieved without it!

Above: Side-loading horseboxes are becoming more popular.

Chapter 8

A question of training... breed versus breed

MOST HORSE lovers have at least one favourite breed. We like to think of our favoured breed as being superior to all others – or else why would we have chosen it? – and most breed enthusiasts like to list the ways in which 'their' breed is superior, usually with reference to its temperament, intelligence, trainability and so on. But how much truth is there in these ideas?

Learning ability

Questions about the learning ability of various breeds are especially difficult to answer, because any judgement is bound to be largely

Right: Appaloosas are supposed to be good learners but need repeated lessons.

Above: Arabian horses are very fast learners and are generally eager to please.

subjective and may depend in part on expectations. We can try to measure how quickly horses of one breed or type learn in comparison with horses of another breed or type. However, we have to be careful, because there are so many variables that can affect learning ability, such as ill health, stress, poor nutrition (especially in early life), management, training, the individual temperament and so on.

Animal behaviour scientist Dr Debbie Marsden states in *How Horses Learn* (J.A. Allen 2005) that 'There is no evidence at all for any differences in rate of learning or 'intelligence' between breeds or types of horses.' However, this is not strictly true. Several authors have found differences in learning ability between horses of various breeds. For example, in one study by D.R. Mader and E.O. Price, a group of Quarter Horses and a group of Thoroughbreds were given discrimination tasks in which they had to learn to distinguish doors with a patterned card on them from other doors each with a different patterned card. The Quarter Horses all completed the task successfully but only 70 per cent of the Thoroughbreds did so. The Quarter Horses also completed the tasks much more quickly than did the Thoroughbreds. These results were documented in *Journal of Animal Science* under the title *Discrimination learning in horses: effects of breed, age and social dominance.*

Does this mean that Quarter Horses are brighter than Thoroughbreds? Not necessarily. Learning ability is affected by emotion and a horse that is under emotional stress may be unable to learn a new task properly because the adrenalin produced by the body to deal with stress increases the amount of input to the brain, effectively bombarding it with information. As a breed, Thoroughbreds tend to be reactive; in other words they are very sensitive to sensory stimuli. They may also be emotional and highly strung. A learning situation that the horse found stressful could well affect the result, as could external factors such as the way the horse was kept. For example, being confined to a stable and fed a ration high in energy (as many Thoroughbreds are) would almost certainly affect the horse's emotional state and therefore its ability to cope with the stress of learning new things.

Below: Miniature horses are reputed to be smart, fast learners.

So it could well be that some differences in learning ability between various breeds are the result of environmental factors rather than genetic ones. Regardless of the breed, we must never lose sight of the fact that the character and temperament of the individual is a product not only of genes but also of environment. Various studies have shown that foals brought up in an environment in which they are allowed to explore, socialize with horses of different ages and of both sexes and in which there are many different things for them to investigate, are likely to be easier to train and manage than those reared in a more restricted environment.

Breed differences

Nevertheless, one can scarcely deny that breed differences do exist. A survey by Karen Hayes, published in 1998 in *Horse and Rider*, under the title *Temperament tip-offs*, cited by K.A. Houpt and R. Kusnose in *Genetics of Behaviour* (*Horse Genetics*, ed. A.T. Bowling and A. Ruvinsky, CABI

Below: Morgans are reputed to be fast learners, easy going, spirited but easily managed.

Publishing, 2000), asked trainers and veterinary surgeons for comments on various characteristics of 10 breeds. These characteristics concerned aspects such as trainability, willingness to work, temperament (behaviour with humans, other horses, non-human animals, for instance), reactions to being asked to do something the horse does not want to do, fearfulness and the animal's impulse to protect itself.

Below: Coloured horses are said to be fast learners but remember that they do not represent a specific breed but come in all types and sizes. This means that there is greater genetic diversity so we should expect a corresponding diversity of character.

Although the replies were based on subjective opinions, in some cases at least the results appear to be pretty accurate assessments of certain breeds. Table 2 on page 135 gives the results obtained from this survey.

These findings indicated that Arabians were the quickest learners – which will come as no surprise to owners of Arabians. My own Arabian horses (five pure-breds and two part-breds, both of the latter having 50 per cent Arabian blood) are all exceptionally quick in the uptake. However, although it can be a pleasure to train such horses, it has its downside: Arabians are just as quick to learn the wrong thing, as they are

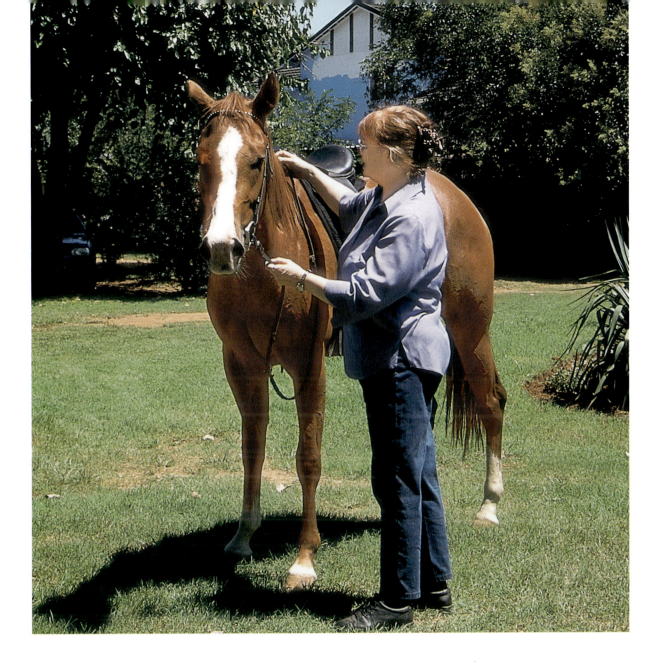

to learn the right thing. This means that you must take extra care and ensure that you do not give the wrong aids, or signals, or inadvertently reward the horse for doing the wrong thing. Of course, this applies to all horses, but especially to Arabians!

The survey findings also tended to confirm those of the study referred to earlier, which found that Quarter Horses were quicker learners than were the Thoroughbreds. Quarter Horses are noted for their patient, easy-going temperaments. Their high tolerance of discomfort and comparatively low reactivity enable them to remain calm in situations that would create stress responses in more reactive types. This unflappability can be a bonus, but it does have its drawbacks. The first time I worked (or attempted to work!) with a Quarter Horse was during a seminar I gave in South Africa in 2002. I was trying to illustrate some

Above: Quarter Horses are quick to learn but may be somewhat unresponsive. I am shown here with a Quarter Horse mare with whom I was attempting to demonstrate a horse's sensitive points!

Above: Warmbloods are the favoured type of horse for dressage, not only because of their size, presence and often spectacular movement, but also because of their phlegmatic temperaments.

of the principles described in Chapter 5, by demonstrating the horse's response to stimulation of the nerves that raise the back and bring the hind legs forward. The mare I was working with was very sweet natured and willing, but she was simply not very responsive. Being accustomed to the instantaneous reactions of our Arabians and their crosses, I found this very frustrating – it was as if she was scarcely aware of my presence! However, I did get a response in the end; I found that I simply had to make my requests in a rather more emphatic way than I would have done with a more sensitive horse.

The same charge has been levelled against Warmbloods. I have often heard people refer to Warmbloods as 'thick', by which they usually mean that the horse is not very responsive. However, as with Quarter Horses, lack of responsiveness may be more a matter of low reactivity, making the horse very 'laid-back'. Much depends on the breeding of individual Warmbloods, though one must remember that there is really no such thing as 'the' Warmblood. The forerunners of the modern Warmbloods were originally bred for cavalry purposes. Native draught types or light

carriage horses were crossed with Spanish horses, Arabians and, later, Thoroughbreds, adding lightness and refinement to the native stock. This resulted in horses of differing types that were nevertheless all characterized by a combination of strength and refinement, power and athleticism, and free elastic movement. Further, highly selective breeding has resulted in the modern sport horses variously called after their place of origin, such as Hanoverian (Saxony, in Germany), Dutch Warmblood (The Netherlands), Belgian and so on.

Above: Saddlebreds may be highly-strung but can be fast learners and willing and affectionate partners.

Because the various Warmblood studbooks are not 'closed' to horses of other breeds, breeders have used outside blood (mostly Thoroughbred, with some Arabian) to continue improving their stock. An increase in the amount of Thoroughbred blood has made many Warmbloods more forward-going than some have been in the past. Nevertheless, the phlegmatic nature of some Warmbloods means that they can be rather backward-thinking and there is no doubt that, like certain Quarter Horses, certain Warmbloods do lack the responsiveness of, say, the Arabian or Thoroughbred. This makes them rather more tolerant of

Opposite: Tennessee Walking Horses may be calm, adaptable and easy going.

forceful or uneducated riding than those breeds. In fact, it is a tribute to their athletic ability that so many of them manage to perform well in spite of some crude and ugly riding! As with Quarter Horses, this phlegmatic temperament makes Warmbloods less likely to become overwrought in the showring than the more reactive types. This, together with their athleticism and the impressive movement possessed by many Warmbloods, has made them pre-eminent in dressage competitions.

It is rather ironic that although there is a common perception in the horse world that the Thoroughbred's conformation and temperament make the breed unsuitable for dressage, many of the most celebrated dressage bloodlines in Warmblood breeding carry an enormous proportion of Thoroughbred blood! In fact, one of the greatest dressage stars of all time, the late Dr Reiner Klimke's Ahlerich (independent and team gold medallist at the 1984 Los Angeles Olympics) was half Thoroughbred, by a German Thoroughbred out of a Westphalian mare.

Below: Standardbreds can be quick learners, easy-going and kind.

While it is true that Thoroughbreds in general may often be too highly strung and sensitive to make good riding horses for nervous or

inexperienced riders, their very sensitivity can, if properly channelled, make them wonderfully responsive to ride. Given that sensitivity, Thoroughbreds adapt to the demands of competition far more readily than one might expect. However, they may find certain situations alarming, but provided their rider knows how to calm their fears, Thoroughbreds can be extremely courageous – a quality which has made them (and cross-bred horses with a high proportion of Thoroughbred blood) the horse of choice for eventing.

Stereotypes and the 'self-fulfilling prophecy'

We have to remember that in any large population there will always be any number that fit the stereotypes. We must also beware of making prior judgements, as expectations regarding specific breeds and types of horse can affect our approach to individual horses, leading to what is often called the self-fulfilling prophecy. For example, a trainer who really believes that horses of a specific breed are difficult to train may very well not make any real effort with a horse of that breed, thinking that it would be a waste of effort. So, of course, the horse does not learn much, and this reinforces the trainer's original prejudice. Yet if that trainer had looked beyond their prejudice, he or she might well have found that the apparent slowness of that horse was a result of other factors – such as the environmental ones referred to earlier in this chapter.

Or, suppose we are told that Thoroughbreds are highly strung. Our attitude towards an individual of that breed may be one of caution in case we upset it. This will be reflected in body language, which the horse will invariably pick up. Some horses may not be concerned by the caution they perceive in our body language, but others may respond with a matching concern: why is the human being cautious? Is there something around that could be dangerous? So the horse will also become cautious and jumpy, which will reinforce our perception that Thoroughbreds are highly strung. This may well be true of some, perhaps many, Thoroughbreds. As I said earlier, as a breed they do tend to be reactive as quick reactions have been selected for in the course of over 300 years of breeding for the racetrack. However, this does not mean that *all* Thoroughbreds are highly strung and easily upset. Much will depend on how the individual horse has been brought up and managed. The best way to approach unfamiliar horses of any breed is to do so calmly and confidently, using neutral body language – that is by not making any sudden movements which the horse may interpret as a threat, but at the same time not being tentative or making fussy little gestures

The best way to approach unfamiliar horses of any breed is to do so calmly and confidently, using neutral body language.

with the hands – and speaking quietly in a friendly tone of voice. Remember, horses are extremely good at reading human body language and vocal intonations!

Every horse is an individual

So, while it can be instructive to learn about breed characteristics, we should never allow preconceived ideas to override the fact that every horse is an individual and as such requires individual treatment. No two horses, no matter what their breeding, will ever react in exactly the same manner. Each horse learns in its own way, and attempts to compel all horses to learn in the same fashion, at the same pace, are doomed to failure. When asked how long it took to train (dress) a horse, the great English master of equitation, William Cavendish, the Duke of Newcastle, replied (as quoted in *A General System of Horsemanship*, a facsimile of the London edition of 1743; J.A. Allen 1970) '...it is very difficult to say in what time a horse may be dressed, because that depends upon his age, strength, spirit and disposition; his agility, memory, sagacity, good or bad temper...It is therefore as impossible to answer this question, as it would be for the ablest master in the world to say, that all the scholars in the university will become learned at a certain time.' – and as an answer, that could scarcely be bettered.

Above: The Thorough-bred's courage as well as its speed makes the breed, together with its close crosses, a favourite for eventing. William Fox-Pitt with TB gelding Birthday Night, Bramham International Three-Day Event, 2005.

Conclusion

Helping horses to cope with our demands

HAVING SEEN how the demands we make of our horses can affect their behaviour and psychological health, we can understand that although horses are extremely adaptable, they are not infinitely so, any more than we are. If we are to fulfil the ethical responsibilities referred to in the Introduction, we may sometimes need to re-evaluate – and in some cases adjust or even abandon – our aims and ideas with regard to our horses.

We can fulfil some of our ethical obligations by considering the effect on horses of frequent moves and changes of ownership, and making any changes as gradual as possible.

We may, for example, pride ourselves on keeping our horses immaculately groomed in well-kept stables with not a piece of hay or straw out of place. This may give pleasure to us and to visitors, but it is meaningless to our horses if they are deprived of those things that do matter to them – freedom to move around, to forage for food, to socialize with other horses – in other words to perform all the behaviours that make them horses. For their sakes, then, we may have to re-think our priorities.

Does it really matter if the horses are not immaculate all the time? Do we need to keep them stabled, or can we find ways of letting them have their freedom while keeping them secure from harm? In some countries it is simply not possible to turn horses out all the year round because of the climate, while in others, where grazing is at a premium, there may be restrictions on turnout. Or, there may be local factors which pose their own problems with regard to letting horses have the freedom they need. Yet in almost every case a little ingenuity can find ways around such problems. For example, a large disused barn could be converted to house horses in an open-plan environment during the winter, allowing them freedom to move around, free access to forage and the company of other horses. Stables could be converted to allow horses to see and touch each other through openings in partition walls, or window openings could be made in back walls of looseboxes to lessen the horse's feeling of being

Left: Horse and human enjoying a mutual scratch.

shut in. Where no suitable equine companions can be provided, sometimes a companion of another species may be the solution. Shatterproof mirrors in stables, because they allow the horse the illusion of companionship, have been found to result in dramatic improvements in horses exhibiting stereotypical behaviour. The provision of ad-lib forage is also a key factor in preventing stable stress – and it is simply not true that horses fed in this way cannot be kept fit!

We can fulfil some of our ethical obligations by considering the effect on horses of frequent moves and changes of ownership, and making any changes as gradual as possible. We can also take a critical look at training methods; are we using punishment inappropriately, for example? Can we make more use of positive reinforcement, and is our use of negative

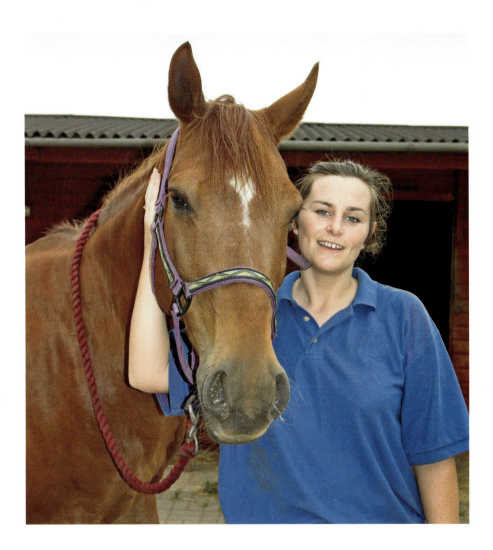

Right: Horse and rider simply having fun in a close relationship.

reinforcement as mild as possible while remaining effective? And are we, in our desire to make progress, perhaps pushing the horse too hard and asking more of it than it is capable of giving at any specific time? Asking these questions and being able to answer them honestly means that we can move on to seek solutions, taking action to anticipate problems and take preventive action before they actually arise.

Sometimes this evaluation process can mean a complete re-think of goals and ambitions.

For instance, suppose you have your heart set on achieving success in some equestrian discipline. You may long for that winner's rosette, but find that your horse simply cannot cope with the demands of your chosen discipline. What can you do? It would be unethical to press ahead regardless, and risk your horse's physical and psychological health by setting it challenges that it simply cannot meet. So you need to re-evaluate your aims. You can either part with your horse and acquire a different one, or you can stand by your equine partner and change your ambitions to suit its capabilities. Either of these decisions could be the right one, depending on the nature of your ambitions and the depth of your relationship with your horse.

Having to change our goals and expectations can be disappointing, but it can also be liberating. Instead of putting pressure on ourselves to achieve success in some discipline or other, or fitting in with other people's ideas of how horses should be trained and managed, we can instead concentrate on the processes of understanding our horses, ensuring that their needs are fulfilled as far as may be possible, making training and riding rewarding for them, and exploring together the possibilities revealed by all those processes.

Below: This horse may be muddy but he does not care; what is far more important to him is being allowed to indulge in normal horse behaviour.

By paying attention to horses' specific needs as *individuals* and allowing them more freedom of choice in how they lead their lives, we can reduce the levels of stress they experience and enable them to deal much better with the demands placed on them by domestication.

Table 1: Lifestyle comparison

Aspect of lifestyle	Horse stabled for all or most of the time	Horse turned out for several hours a day, stable the rest of the time, fed ad-lib hay or other forage	Horse turned out 24 hours a day, 7 days a week, all year round	Free-ranging horse existing as part of a group in a large area with set boundaries (such as ponies living in the New Forest in England)	Feral horse living in family group in a large unpopulated area
Free access to forage	None, may be limited to a small amount of hay twice (rarely more) a day	Increased access to forage but still limited by the amount of time out	Unlimited access to forage, may suffer shortage in winter, depending on climate	Unlimited access to forage, may suffer shortage in winter, depending on climate	Unlimited access to forage, may suffer shortage in winter, depending on climate
Freedom of movement	Opportunities for movement limited to time spent outside the stable in work, or to the amount of space the horse has inside the stable	Freedom of movement limited by the amount of time horse is turned out and the size of the turnout area	Freedom of movement limited only by the size of the turnout area	Unlimited freedom of movement within set boundaries	Unlimited freedom of movement
Social contact	None, unless the horse is kept in a stable which enables him to see and touch his neighbours	Limited amount of social contact, determined by the number of hours out (and with whom: he may be turned out alone)	If turned out with other horses, unlimited opportunity for social contact	Unlimited opportunities for social contact	Unlimited opportunities for social contact
Group stability giving emotional security	Not applicable	Horse may be turned out with the same companions every day, or companions may change, stability may be therefore be uncertain	Companions may remain the same or may change regularly, stability may be uncertain	Unless regularly interfered with by humans, greater social stability is likely	Although the structure of family bands does change over time, these changes are likely to be gradual (see Chapter 3). Greater social stability usually the norm
Opportunity to form close bonds of friendship and affection with other horses	Non-existent except where there is limited contact with neighbours	Where horses are turned out with the same companions every day, bonds may form; frequent changes of companions may prevent formation of close bonds	Where horses are turned out with the same companions every day, bonds may form, frequent changes of companions may prevent formation of close bonds	Unless horses are taken out of/added to the group, strong bonds are likely to form	The members of most family bands form strong, long-term social bonds

Table 2: Survey of different breeds

This table first appeared in Horse & Rider magazine (US), 1998

Breed	Trainability (ability to learn new tasks)	Work ethic (willingness to perform repetitive work or tasks already well-learned: stamina in the face of fatigue)	Temperament	When asked to do something the horse does not want to do	Fearfulness (in response to benign stimuli such as unexpected noise or movement)	Flight (in response to benign stimuli such as unexpected noise or movement)	Response to pain
Appaloosa	Good learner but needs lessons repeated	Needs incentive: does not like change in routine	Easy going, inquisitive	Acts dumb; passive aggressive	Low	Low	High: self protection
Arabian	Fastest learner	Energetic	Easily bored, playful, impressionable	Eager to please but evades	Over-reactive	High	Inconsistent; can be extremely self-protective or extremely tolerant
Miniature Horse	Fast learner, smart	Hardworker, not lazy	Highly strung	Stubborn	Average	Average	High
Morgan	Good, fast learner	Willing, diligent	Easy going, spirited but easily managed	Adaptable and compliant	Not easily frightened	Low	Low; tolerates pain
Paint Horse	Fast learner	Hard worker	Reasonable, easy going	Does it anyway	Average	Average (Tobiano low, Overo high)	Average
Quarter Horse	Fast, reasonable	Patient, compliant	Easy going	Does what it is asked	Not reactive	Low	Average or below
American Saddlebred	Fast, receptive	Willing, hard worker	Highly strung, personable, affectionate, plays with stall toys	Compliant, eager to please	Easily frightened	Low	Slightly above average
Standardbred	Fast learner	Obedient	Easy going, level headed, kind	Gives in	Low, sensible	Low	Low
Tennessee Walking Horse	Good	Not enthusiastic	Good, calm, adaptable, easy going	Does it anyway	Unflappable	Low	Low
Thoroughbred	Reasonably fast but lacks ability to concentrate	Hard worker	Highly strung, emotional, reactive	May react with fearfulness, refusal, does it anyway	High	High	High

Glossary

Aversive stimulus – a stimulus the subject wishes to avoid.

Behaviour – the response of an organism to a specific stimulus or group of stimuli. In practical terms, it covers virtually everything an animal does.

Cavalletti – supports shaped in the form of an X on which poles can be raised for the horse to step over in walk, trot or canter. The X is usually formed so that the height of the poles can be varied slightly.

Cavesson – a type of padded noseband with rings attached to the front and sides, nowadays used mainly for lunging and long-reining but in the seventeenth and eighteenth centuries widely used like a kind of bitless bridle. The bit would only be introduced when the horse was ready for it, usually when the canine teeth had come through.

Classical Equitation – riding and training based on principles established over many centuries, in which the aim is to restore the horse's natural balance and enhance his paces under saddle by working in harmony with his physical and psychological nature. Truly classical trainers and riders reject the use of force.

Claustrophobia – an abnormal fear of enclosed spaces. Horses are often described as claustrophobic when in fact their fear of enclosed spaces is a normal equine response. Some horses, however, may experience this fear in an extreme form which could be described as claustrophobia.

Clicker – a small box containing a metal strip which when pressed makes a clicking noise.

Clicker-training – training which makes use of the clicker as a 'marker' to tell an animal the exact point at which it has done what the human wanted.

Colic – acute spasmodic abdominal pain. Horses suffering from colic often roll to try to alleviate this pain.

Conditioning – a learning process in which an event occurring within an animal's environment acts to modify the animal's behaviour.

Dominance hierarchy – the order in which animals in a specific group have priority of access to resources such as food, water, mates and so on. This order is usually determined by observers on the basis of the number of aggressive acts carried out by specific animals, and other animals' responses to such acts. There is a great deal of confusion regarding horses and dominance hierarchies, and assumptions are often made without sufficient supporting evidence.

Duke of Newcastle – William Cavendish, 1st Duke of Newcastle (1592-1676): English soldier, politician and writer. He was one of the most influential masters of equitation of his time.

Ecological knowledge – an animal's knowledge of its environment, for example where to find food and shelter, places and foods to avoid, possible locations of predators, and so on.

Endocrine glands – glands which manufacture hormones that are released directly into the bloodstream.

Eocene epoch – a period of geological time extending from about 54 million years ago to about 38 million years ago. Many groups of mammals first appeared in the Eocene, including rodents, carnivores, whales and the early ancestors of camels and horses.

Equid – any member of the family *Equidae*, or horse family. This includes true horses such as the domestic horse (*Equus caballus*), Przewalskiís horse, zebras and asses.

Equus caballus – the domestic horse

Equus przewalskii – a wild horse last recorded in the wild in 1947. *E. przewalskii* was once thought to be the direct ancestor of modern horses, but DNA testing has shown that this is not the case. However *E. przewalskii* and *E. caballus* do descend from common ancestors.

Extinction – when behaviour ceases because it is not being reinforced, it is said to have become extinct.

Feral – animals living in a wild state, that are descended from domestic animals.

Gregarious animals – animals living together in groups.

Habituation – growing accustomed to a situation or stimulus to the point that these no longer produce a significant response.

High School – the highest level of training of the horse, which includes the extremely collected gaits, *piaffe*, *passage*, and the jumps such as the *capriole*.

Home range – an area normally occupied by a group of animals; unlike a territory, a home range is not defended.

Horse whisperer – term used to describe the 19th century horseman Dan Sullivan, who was supposed to be able to tame an unmanageable horse by whispering in its ear. The term is now often loosely applied to anyone who has a way of managing difficult horses, and people who practise 'natural horsemanship' are sometimes referred to as 'horse whisperers'.

Immune system – the body's system of protection against disease.

Natural horsemanship – a collective term for a number of training methods which vary greatly in their approach, but which are all based on communication with the horse using body language (supposedly of the kind the horse understands). The idea is that the horse will respond willingly rather than having to be coerced. A number of assumptions (not all of them accurate) are built into this philosophy and although Natural Horsemanship methods are now very popular, an increasing number of people are questioning the thinking behind them. Nevertheless there are a number of gifted trainers using Natural Horsemanship methods sympathetically and effectively.

Negative reinforcement – conditioning which relies on the removal of a stimulus to act as a reinforcer (see under Reinforcer).

Negative reward – the removal of a stimulus, e.g. easing of pressure on a headcollar.

Neurotransmitters – chemicals that enable

nerve impulses to be transmitted from one nerve cell to another.

Passage – a cadenced, elevated trot in which the moment of suspension is clearly defined.

Pecking order – a dominance hierarchy in which a subordinate always responds to aggression with submission. First described in chickens (hence the term 'pecking order') by the Norwegian naturalist Schjelderup-Ebbe in the 1920s.

Personal space – the distance separating members of the same species.

Piaffe – 'a *passage* in place' (definition given by the 18th century French master of equitation François Robichon de la Guérinière).

Positive reinforcement – conditioning which relies on the addition of something the subject finds pleasing or rewarding, to act as a reinforcer.

Positive reward – the addition of something the subject finds pleasant or rewarding.

Punishment – an action aimed at preventing a specific behaviour, either by the addition of something the subject finds unpleasant or painful (positive punishment) or the removal of something the subject likes or wants (negative punishment).

Reflexes – rapid, automatic responses to specific stimuli.

Reinforcement – the act of reinforcing a behaviour.

Reinforcer – anything that tends to make the subject repeat an action or behaviour.

Schools of Classical Horsemanship – academies of equitation where classical horsemanship is practised for its own sake rather than as a means to competitive success. Examples are: the Portuguese School of Equestrian Art, Reitinstitut von Neindorff in Germany, the Cadre Noir in France and, of course, the world-famous Spanish Riding School in Vienna.

Shaping – building desired behaviour by breaking it down into steps and reinforcing approximations of the behaviour, progressing to reinforcing only when the subject offers an even closer approximation, until the desired result is achieved.

Shoulder-in – a lateral exercise designed to improve suppleness and encourage engagement of the hind legs.

Socially naïve – an animal inexperienced in social interaction.

Stereotypy – a fixed, repetitive, apparently meaningless action, e.g. head-nodding, weaving, box-walking.

Stimulus – an object or event that is perceived by the senses.

Variable schedule of reinforcement – a programme of reinforcement in which the desired behaviour is not reinforced every time, but intermittently.

Xenophon – Greek historian, philosopher and cavalry commander (c.444 BC to c.357 BC). As well as numerous historical and philosophical works, he wrote the famous treatise on horsemanship *Peri hippikes* (usually translated as *The Art of Horsemanship*).

Recommended reading

BECAUSE HUMANS interact with horses in so many different ways, we need to understand what happens when we ride them as well as how they behave without a rider. For this reason I have included a number of books on riding and schooling, because they all give insight into the horse-rider interaction. I have also included a book on how dogs learn, simply because the only book on my list which might have explained in depth how horses learn is seriously flawed with regard to learning principles! I have given some brief comments on certain books which I felt needed remarking on in some way, and I have marked those of special value or interest with an asterisk*

Blignault, Karin *Successful Schooling*,
J. A. Allen 1997
*Burch, Mary R. and Bailey, Jon S. *How Dogs Learn*, Howell Book House 1999
Although this is about dogs, it gives some excellent explanations of the learning process and the principles of conditioning and reinforcement.
*Hogg, Abigail *The Horse Behaviour Handbook*, David & Charles 2003
Kiley-Worthington, Dr Marthe *Equine Welfare*,
J. A. Allen 1997
*Kiley-Worthington, Dr Marthe *Horse Watch: What it is to be Equine*, J. A. Allen 2005
The most comprehensive non-academic book available on equine behaviour.
Kiley-Worthington, Dr Marthe *The Behaviour of Horses*, J. A. Allen 1987
*Loch, Sylvia *Invisible Riding*, Horse's Mouth Publications 2003
Loch, Sylvia *The Classical Seat*, Horse's Mouth Publications 2003

Explains with great clarity the correct way to sit on a horse.
MacLeay, Jennifer M. *Smart Horse: Understanding the Science of Natural Horsemanship*, Eclipse Press 2003
Clear and concise explanations of the principles of conditioning and reinforcement.
Marsden, Dr Debbie *How Horses Learn*,
J. A. Allen 2005
Contains some excellent chapters on how the brain works, the learning process and how brain chemistry affects learning, habituation, de-sensitizing and retraining techniques, as well as some very helpful case-histories which explain how certain problem behaviours arise. However the book's value is lessened by the author's confusion of negative reinforcement with punishment.
Mills, Daniel and Nankervis, Kathryn *Equine Behaviour: Principles and Practice* Blackwell Publishing 1999
Pryor, Karen *Don't Shoot the Dog!*, (Revised ed.) Bantam 1999
This ground-breaking book explains the power of positive reinforcement.
*Rees, Lucy *The Horse's Mind*, Stanley Paul 1984
An insightful and inspiring look at equine behaviour.
*Skipper, Lesley *Let Horses Be Horses*,
J. A. Allen 2005
Skipper, Lesley *Realize Your Horse's True Potential*, J. A. Allen 2003
*Wyche, Sara *The Anatomy of Riding*, Crowood Press 2004
Explains the horse-rider interaction with great clarity, using excellent drawings to illustrate the text.

Useful organizations and websites

THERE ARE now so many equestrian organizations worldwide that it is impossible to list more than a very small number of them. I have included here only those known to me personally and which appear to offer the most to people wanting to improve their understanding of equine behaviour as well as their riding and general horse management skills.

The Equine Behaviour Forum

The Equine Behaviour Forum is a voluntary, non-profit-making, international group of people interested in equine behaviour. Its members come from a very wide range of backgrounds and include vets, scientists, professional and amateur horse people, breeders, casual riders and horse owners, serious competitors and also people who have no access to equines or who simply prefer to observe them. The EBF produces a journal, *Equine Behaviour*, edited by author Susan McBane, which includes members' letters, articles, views and experiences, some scientific papers, book reviews and much more.

• Membership Secretary: Ms Gillian Cooper,
50 Marsh House Lane, Over Darwen,
Lancashire, England, BB3 3JB, UK.
Tel: + 44 (0)1254-705487.
Website: www.gla.ac.uk/external/EBF/

The Classical Riding Club

The Classical Riding Club was started in 1995 by internationally renowned trainer, writer and lecturer Sylvia Loch as a means of bringing together like-minded people who were interested in a more philosophical approach to riding, which puts the happiness and wellbeing of the horse above all else. The Classical Riding Club's membership is truly international and includes people with widely differing equestrian backgrounds and levels of ability. Members receive a quarterly newsletter which contains instructional articles, book reviews, members' letters and articles by members as well as details of demonstrations, seminars, open days, teach-ins, lectures etc. Membership of the CRC also gives members access to a general equestrian helpline, as well as expert advice via the network of regional liaison members. There is also a list, available at a nominal charge, of trainers/instructors who have signed a declaration to say they promise to teach under the classical principles and ethos as laid down in the Club's Charter.

• The Classical Riding Club
Eden Hall, Kelso, Roxburghshire, TD5 7QD, UK.
Fax: + 44 (0)1890 830667
Email: crc@classicalriding.co.uk
Website: www.classicalriding.co.uk

The Intelligent Horsemanship Association

This was founded by Kelly Marks, a pupil of Monty Roberts and the first teacher of his methods worldwide. It is an organization dedicated to bringing together the best horsemanship ideas from around the world in an effort to promote understanding and fair treatment of horses at every opportunity.

• The Intelligent Horsemanship Association
Lethornes, Lambourn, Hungerford, Berkshire RG17 8QS, England.
Tel: + 44 (0)1488 71300
Fax: + 44 (0)1488 73783.
Email: kelly@montyroberts.co.uk
Website: www.intelligenthorsemanship.co.uk

The Company of Horses

The Company of Horses website contains a wealth of information on Emma Kurrels' and Ben Hart's research and work with equine intelligence, learning abilities and innate behaviour.

• Contact: Emma Kurrels, Dolfallt Isaf, Rhandirmwym, Llandovery, Carmarthen, South Wales, SA20 0NH, UK

Tel: +44 (0) 1550 760363

Email: learn@companyofhorses.com

Website: www.companyofhorses.com

Why Does My Horse

The Why Does My Horse website expresses the ideas and beliefs of a group of like-minded people. Their vision is to empower horse owners to make informed decisions about equine management and training. On this site you will find information on 'normal' horse behaviour and ethology, alternative methods of horse management, training and holistic management approaches to equine behavioural problems.

Website: www.whydoesmyhorse.co.uk

Thinking Horsemanship Forum

The Thinking Horsemanship Forum is for anyone (beginner, professional or somewhere in-between) who would like to understand more about the behaviour of horses (and other animals) and how they learn.

Website: www.network54.com/Forum/235380/

Damelin Equestrian Academy

The Damelin Equestrian Academy was launched in October 2001 on the site of Codi Stud, an American Quarter Horse Stud. The Equestrian Centre includes the stud farm and farrier workshop together with superb equine training facilities, from dressage arenas to show jumping arenas. The Equestrian centre provides a complete solution to both academic and practical tuition in the field of equine sciences, including equine behaviour. The use of specialist instructors and the close relationship with SANEF (South Africa National Equestrian Federation), offers learners exemplary qualifications with superb surroundings.

Website:www.damelin.co.za/home/welcome.asp

Horse Junction

Excellent source of equestrian information for South Africa.

Website: www.horsejunction.co.za

Jayne Lavender Natural Horsemanship in Australia

Jayne has influenced British trainer Charles Wilson, whose work is illustrated in photographs appearing in Chapters 4 and 5 of this book.

Website: www.uk-website.co.uk/jayne/index.php

Jessica Jahiel

Jessica Jahiel's HORSE-SENSE Newsletter is a free, subscriber-supported electronic Q&A newsletter which deals with all aspects of horses, their management, riding and training. Since 1995, Jessica Jahiel, award-winning author, clinician, and lecturer, has been writing 8–12 articles a month based on questions from subscribers. Over 1375 articles are currently indexed and searchable in the newsletter archives.

Website: www.horse-sense.org/

Horsebox and trailer manufacturers

Website: www.animaltransportation.com/

Index

Picture credits

KEY
Copyright rests with the photographers and/or their agents.
BL = Bob Langrish
TG = Telané Greyling
LS = Lesley Skipper
NHP = New Holland Publishers

Key to locations: t = top; b = bottom; l = left; r = right; c = centre